Nikolai Bukharin

Nikolai Bukharin

The Last Years

———»»«««———

ROY A. MEDVEDEV

Translated by A. D. P. Briggs

W·W·NORTON & COMPANY

New York · London

FIRST EDITION

>>> THE TEXT *of this book is composed in photocomposition Caledonia. Display type used is Perpetua and Garamond. Composition and manufacturing are by the Maple-Vail Book Manufacturing Group. Book design is by Marjorie J. Flock.*

Library of Congress Cataloging in Publication Data
Medvedev, Roy Aleksandrovich.
    Nikolai Bukharin: the last years.
    Includes bibliographical references and index.
    1. Bukharin, Nikolai Ivanovich, 1888–1938.
    2. Statesmen—Russia—Biography.   3. Revolutionists—
Russia—Biography.   I. Title.
DK268.B76M42   1980   947.084'092'4 [B]   80–14287

ISBN 0–393–01357–X

W. W. Norton & Company, Inc. 500 Fifth Avenue, New York, N.Y. 10110
W. W. Norton & Company Ltd. 25 New Street Square, London EC4A 3 NT

1 2 3 4 5 6 7 8 9 0

Contents

———————— »» ««————————

Foreword

———— »»«« ————

IN THE SOVIET UNION Bukharin's name is still banned.
Even in the recently reissued *Great Soviet Encyclopedia* and in the
Soviet Historical Encyclopedia there is no article on Bukharin, no
mention of him at all. And yet we are speaking of one of the most
eminent leaders and theoreticians of the Bolsheviks, a man who had
become deservedly famous long before the Revolution. In 1917
Bukharin was one of the most prominent organizers of the October
Revolution in Moscow. For twenty years he served on the Central
Committee of the Bolshevik party and for ten years he was a
member of the Politburo. From 1917 to 1929 Bukharin was in
charge of the central organ of the Party, the newspaper *Pravda*.
Lenin frequently took issue with Bukharin, but nevertheless he did
not fail to acknowledge him as "a splendidly educated Marxist
economist" whose errors stemmed largely from his attempt to
"think through the specific difficulties of the transition—that agonis-
ing and arduous transition—from capitalism to socialism."[1] Bukharin was referred to by Lenin in his *Testament* as "the greatest and
most valuable theoretician in the Party," and "deservedly the
favourite of the Party." Despite the frequent disagreements between them, Lenin himself treated Bukharin with unusual affection,
almost like a son. During Lenin's fatal illness Bukharin spent more
time in conversation with him than anyone else. When Lenin died,
his sister Maria Ulyanova chose Bukharin as the person to be first
informed.

After Lenin's death Nikolai Ivanovich Bukharin became without a doubt the leading theorist of the Party. It was Bukharin who used to draft what everyone then called "the general Party line." Bukharin was the chief of staff of the Bolshevik army commanded by Stalin. It was natural that the so-called leftist opposition of the period sometimes spoke out more decisively against Bukharin than against Stalin. Trotsky is reputed to have said, "Lining up with Stalin against Bukharin—yes, that's possible. Lining up with Bukharin against Stalin—never."

"The best of the Party theorists," "the best of all Party workers," "a man loved by us all whom we shall continue to support"—all this was said of Bukharin at the Fourteenth Party Congress by Ordzhonikidze, Molotov, Stalin, and other speakers. One unofficial Soviet historian wrote some years ago: "In the twentieth-century chronicle of revolution the name of Nikolai Ivanovich Bukharin may justly be described as the first after Lenin's." This estimate is, of course, something of an exaggeration but it contains a significant grain of truth.

A section of the middle generation of our country still associates the name of Bukharin with such concepts as "an enemy of the people," "traitor," and so on. This, after all, was exactly what our press wrote about him for almost twenty years before the Twentieth Party Congress. However, the younger generation which has grown up after that congress is almost entirely ignorant of Bukharin. All they know is that Bukharin was the leader of the "Left Communists" who opposed the Treaty of Brest-Litovsk in 1918 but that within ten years, in 1928, that same Bukharin had become leader of the "rightist" opposition resisting forced collectivization and the liquidation of the kulaks.

A small amount of information on Bukharin, the essential minimum for present-day propagandists, is to be found in the Index of Names in Lenin's *Complete Works*. This entry is worth setting out here in full:

BUKHARIN, N. I. (1888–1938): Bolshevik party member from 1906; worked on propaganda in various parts of Moscow. Emigrated in 1911. In 1915 worked on the journal *Communist*, taking a non-Marxist line on ques-

tions of the state, the dictatorship of the proletariat, on the right of nations `
to self-determination, etc. At the Sixth Party Congress produced an anti-
Leninist scheme for the development of the Revolution based on rejection
of the union between the working class and the impoverished peasantry.
Following the October Revolution—editor of *Pravda*, member of the Comintern Executive Committee. Frequent opponent of the Party's Leninist
policy: in 1918 head of the anti-Lenin group of "Left Communists," during
Party discussions of trade unions adopted first a "buffer" stance before joining Trotsky group, head of Party rightist opposition from 1928. Removed
from Central Committee Politburo in 1929. Expelled from Party ranks in
1937 for anti-Party activities.[2]

It is not our purpose in the present book to refute this entry and
detail Bukharin's multifarious revolutionary and political activities.
Over the last ten years the figure of Bukharin has been attracting
the interest of an ever-increasing number of foreign historians.
Among the books published in the West in the 1960s and '70s on the
subject of Bukharin's views and ultimate fate one might mention
George Katkov's study, *The Trial of Bukharin* (Batsford, London
1969) and A. G. Löwy's *Die Weltgeschichte ist das Weltgericht,
Bucharin : Vision des Kommunismus* (Europa Verlag, Wien-
Frankfurt-Zürich 1969). In 1972 and 1973 the Italian Communist
party publishing house Riuniti issued two large collections of
documents on the history of the CPSU in which the works of
Bukharin occupy a prominent place. (N. Bucharin–E. Preobrazen-
skij, *L'accumulazione socialista*, Rome 1972; and Bucharin, Stalin,
Trotskij, Zinovjev, *La "Rivoluzione Permanente" e il socialismo in
um Paese Solo*, Rome 1973.) The most valuable and substantial work
on Bukharin is without doubt the large volume written by the
American historian Stephen F. Cohen, *Bukharin and the Bolshevik
Revolution: A Political Biography, 1888–1938* (Knopf, New York
1973). On the one hand this book may be said to answer the needs of
the growing interest in Bukharin as a revolutionary figure, politician, and theorist; on the other hand, it also increases the interest
by opening up the possibilities of further research.

This is not to mention the large number of articles on Bukharin
in newspapers and journals—it is well known that a particularly
wide-ranging and impassioned discussion of Bukharin unfolded in

the pages of the Western press during 1978. One foreign researcher, Sidney Heitman, the compiler of a collection of selected works by Bukharin, wrote as follows in substantiation of the interest shown by historians and political commentators in the activities and the personality of Bukharin:

Alone among all of Lenin's successors, he enjoyed not only great authority and influence as a political leader and theoretician, but also immense personal popularity with both the leaders and the rank and file of the Party, . . . Bukharin's personal appeal rested on his open simplicity, sincerity, and integrity. Though undistinguished in appearance, his personal warmth and congeniality touched all who knew him. A ready wit, sharp tongue, and facile mind overshadowed his simple dress, retiring manner, and frequently detached air. He lived a spartan, almost monk-like existence, worked exceedingly long and irregular hours and cared little for the material comforts or amenities of life. Having separated from his first wife in the early nineteen-twenties, he devoted all his waking hours to the Party and to ceaseless study. He devoured books in several languages, and could discuss with professorial authority the entire spectrum of twentieth century thought. Most particularly, he was idolized by the youth of Soviet Russia, who identified with him and drew much of their intellectual inspiration from his writings. During the later nineteen-twenties Bukharin had only to step up to a speaker's podium at the numerous meetings he attended to touch off long and boisterous ovations, and the recorded accounts of his speeches invariably note tumultuous demonstrations following their conclusion. Except for Lenin, with whom Bukharin was often favorably compared by Communists and non-Communists observers alike, no other individual in the Party's history until that time occupied so universally popular a place.

At the same time, he also commanded during these years (after the defeat of Trotsky) greater authority in the Communist world than any of Lenin's successors. At the peak of his career, Bukharin held leading positions in numerous Party, Soviet and Comintern organizations, including the Central Committee and the Politburo of the Russian Communist Party, the Central Executive Committee and the Presidium of the Congress of Soviets, the central organs of the Comintern, of which he became chairman in 1926, succeeding Zinoviev, the Komsomol, the Central Council of Trade Unions, the Red International of Trade Unions, the Institute of Red Professors, the Communist Academy, the Institute of Marx-Engels-Lenin, and a multitude of other policy-making and administrative organizations concerned with political, economic, social, cultural, scientific, and educational affairs. Throughout the nineteen-twenties, moreover, he was a leading delegate and speaker at every Party and Comintern congress, where he played a dominant role in shaping decisions and formulating their official pronouncements. His authority and influence were further heightened by his post as editor of *Pravda*, which he held continuously from 1917 to 1929, with the exception of a brief interval during 1918.

In retrospect, however, it should be noted that notwithstanding his attainment of some of the highest offices in the Soviet and international Communist hierarchy, Bukharin's most significant and enduring impact on the evolution of Bolshevism resulted not from the manipulation of the instruments and symbols of power, but rather from the force of his thought. Bukharin was first and foremost an intellectual. For him, the struggle of communism had to be waged not only on the barricades, but also in the minds of men, and it was to this latter task that he devoted his major effort. Possessed of a keen mind, perhaps second only to that of Trotsky, amazing erudition unmatched by any other Party leader, and a facile pen, he was regarded in his day as the ablest and most versatile thinker in the Party by Communists and non-Communists alike. His views on a multitude of problems confronting the Bolshevik leadership before and after 1917 exerted a greater impact on the ideology of the Party than those of any other individual, except Lenin. As a theoretical economist, Bukharin had no peer in the Communist world, and his pioneering studies and reformulations of Marxist economic doctrine became Party classics during his lifetime. Through his writings on such diverse subjects as philosophy, sociology, political theory, psychology, natural science, literature, art and education, moreover he was instrumental in directing the Party's efforts to develop a Marxist foundation for the conceptual and methodological problems in these areas. Finally, as the author of literally hundreds of books, pamphlets, and articles, as a frequent speaker at innumerable Party, Soviet, and Comintern meetings, and as a regular participant in scores of other specialized and mass organisations, he not only helped to shape, but also to disseminate and popularize current Bolshevik thought within the Party, among the non-Party masses, and beyond the Soviet Union. Lenin's well-known testamentary characterization of Bukharin as the Party's 'most valuable and most important theoretician' was almost universally shared throughout the Russian and international Communist movement, and it was with justification that observers within and outside Soviet Russia considered him the foremost leader of his day and the legitimate heir and successor of Lenin.[3]

This book describes the events of the last years of Bukharin's life. These events are passed over in complete silence by the "biographical notice" quoted above, and many details have never before been available to foreign researchers working on Bukharin.

Nikolai Bukharin

One

On the Threshold of a New Decade

———— »» ««« ————

DURING THE NIGHT OF 1 January 1930 a knock came at the door of Stalin's flat in the Kremlin. Stalin, merry from New Year celebrations with his friends, went to open the door to the new guests, uninvited as they were. Three men stood on the threshold, holding bottles of wine—Nikolai Bukharin, Aleksei Rykov, and Mikhail Tomsky. They had come to Stalin for a friendly reconciliation.

The brief, though at times rather bitter, struggle with the so-called rightist faction was to all intents and purposes finished: Stalin had won. For Stalin this struggle, which had taken place at first exclusively within the Politburo, was in many respects more difficult than the one with the "leftist" opposition. Bukharin had insisted on the continuation and development of the New Economic Policy, the basic features of which had been worked out by Lenin. Lenin wrote that NEP was being introduced in the country "in a serious manner and for a long time," and that NEP must be the very means by which the Party was to build a socialist society in the backward, peasants' country that was Russia. This was why Bukharin, Rykov, and Tomsky had come out against extending the extraordinary measure proposed by Stalin to deal with the kulaks, against enforced collectivization, against gigantism in building up industry—all of which in fact represented a rejection of the New Economic Policy. No one could know in advance where Stalin's new course would lead the Party and the country, nor how this sudden new "revolution from above" would work out and what consequences it might have.

There was no doubt that the difficulties over grain procurement which arose in the autumn of 1927 and which worsened in 1928 were extremely serious. The problems that did arise were related to a whole series of errors in economic policy made during 1925 and 1926, and Nikolai Bukharin was one who played an active part in the formulation of that policy. Grain prices fixed by the state proved to be too low. On the other hand, the premature reduction of prices for many industrial goods and the lowering of the agricultural tax, together with the rise in fixed prices for many industrial crops—all these factors led to a significant drop in voluntary sales of grain by the countryside to the state. The measures proposed by Stalin, particularly the requisitioning of grain from the kulaks, brought about some improvement in the grain balance and in supplies to the cities. But these measures met with opposition from the kulaks, middle peasants, and large sections of the Party and soviet workers. Objections came also from Party economists and budgetary experts. Nikolai Bukharin supported the use of extraordinary measures at first, but soon realized the enormous risks in continuing with such a policy. He suggested that it be renounced and that new economic means be found to survive the crisis. A rise in grain purchasing prices and in the agricultural tax, and an increase in production of goods intended for the country, would take the pressure off. In order to stop kulak sabotage and guarantee bread supplies for the cities Bukharin proposed a temporary reduction in allocations for building up heavy industry and the purchasing abroad of some of the grain needed to feed the cities. The production of industrial goods needed for the countryside would have to be increased and some of these, according to Bukharin, would have to be imported from abroad. All these measures would help solve the impending crisis in economic and political affairs—but without recourse to violence. The growth in the production of agricultural and consumer goods would allow resources to accumulate, and in turn lead to a speedy restoration of the planned development of heavy industry.

As to collectivization, Bukharin insisted that the fairly moderate pace envisioned in the Five-Year Plan must be adhered to. The enforcement of collectivization, the setting up of tens of thousands of collective farms without the benefit of the latest technology or financial backing by the state, or of leadership experience in collective methods, seemed to Bukharin a very risky business; instead of raising agricultural production, it might lead to a decline.

At first, Bukharin's proposals were supported by a majority in the Politburo. Finding himself in the minority, Stalin played for time. For the first time in many years he left his study not for a holiday in the Caucasus but to travel out to Siberia where there were particularly heavy grain surpluses and yet where grain procurement was remarkably low. Stalin spent some time in Novosibirsk and Barnaul, visiting particular regions and chatting with workers and peasants. He returned from this journey in a state of extreme irritation; he had realized that hardly any of the Party or soviet workers shared his point of view. This was his last trip out of town; to the end of his days Stalin never visited the countryside again. His element was the realm of political infighting, and this was where he now concentrated all his efforts. And admission of error was out of the question. Playing on the fact that Bukharin and Rykov had limited themselves for the most part to polemical discussion within the Politburo, Stalin went about denying publicly the existence of any disagreement within the Politburo, and throughout the whole of 1928 he made only vague references to dangers "from the right" or of "rightist" deviation. However, in late 1928 Stalin managed to win Kalinin and Voroshilov over to his side. Now, with a majority in the Politburo supporting him, Stalin made a sudden attack on Bukharin at the plenary session of the Central Committee in January 1929. He spoke as follows:

Comrades! However regrettably, we must acknowledge the fact that a special Bukharin group has been formed within our Party, consisting of Bukharin, Tomsky, and Rykov. The existence of this group has hitherto been unknown to the Party—Bukharin's men have taken good care to hide the existence of their group from the Party. Now, however, it has become known and clear to all of us. This group, as is obvious from its own declared position, possesses its own particular platform which it has set up in opposition to Party policy. . . .[1]

This statement was untrue, since it was Stalin in the first instance, and not Bukharin, who had gone to great lengths to hide from the Party the existence of serious differences of opinion with the Politburo. Even more erroneous and inaccurate was Stalin's exposition of the attitudes of Bukharin and his like-minded colleagues. However, still uncertain of general support within the Central Committee and wishing to avoid dragging all the thorny problems out into the open for judgment by the Party as a whole, Stalin proposed withholding the details of the January–February (1929) plenary session of the Central Committee from publication. Certain extracts from Stalin's speeches at that session were to be published for the first time in the second volume of his *Collected Works* in 1949.

The period from January to April 1929 was to prove decisive in the conflict between Bukharin's faction (and political line) and Stalin's. This conflict expressed itself mainly in the form of bitter exchanges within the Politburo, as, for example, at the meetings of the Politburo and the Central Committee presidium on 30 January and 9 February of that year. Party activists learned of these discussions via special restricted letters from the Politburo in which the position of the country and the upper echelons of the Party was given a very biased presentation.

Bukharin was anything but an expert in Party infighting. Stalin, however, began with an attack on the kulaks and the New Economic Policy in general, and went on to seek contact with the feared leadership of the "leftist" opposition (naturally excluding Trotsky). Zinoviev and Kamenev were restored to the ranks of the Party. One after another the "leftist" leaders who had been dispatched just recently to the provinces began to return to Moscow where they received positions of responsibility. They included, among others, Georgi Piatakov, V. Antonov-Ovseyenko, E. Preobrazhensky, K. Radek, I. T. Smilga, L. P. Serebriakov, and I. N. Smirnov. Meanwhile, Bukharin's attempt to contact Kamenev in order to discuss the Party's

new situation was immediately condemned as an attempt to establish another anti-Party faction, as a step toward the break-up of
the Party, and so on.

Earlier than this, in the autumn of 1928, Bukharin had published
an article in *Pravda* entitled "Notes of an Economist" which set out
in detail a plan to solve the country's economic difficulties without
further "revolutions" by updating and extending NEP. In this article Bukharin spoke out in favor of limiting the activities of the
kulaks, developing cooperation, and conducting a more sensible
pricing policy. He defended the principle of a planned economy but
stressed the dangers of taking planning to outrageous extremes
since it was impossible to predict every single contingency. Industrial planning must keep pace with the development of agriculture,
he reasoned, and must take into account the actual resources possessed by the country. Industrialization was not to be achieved at
the cost of a reduction in agricultural output; the pace of industrialization must be a reasonable one; and an increase in productivity must be given high priority, together with a lowering of costs.

At the time of the article's appearance, Stalin refrained from taking issue with Bukharin. He even went so far as to state in one of his
speeches that Bukharin had presented a series of theoretical questions that were "quite feasible and reasonable."[2]

At the end of January 1929 it fell to Bukharin to speak to a meeting called to mark the fifth anniversary of Lenin's death. In his
address, entitled "The Political Testament of Lenin," Bukharin gave
a detailed exposition of Lenin's views on the future prospects for the
building of socialism in the USSR, based on articles and speeches by
Vladimir Ilyich in 1921 and 1922. Anyone listening to or reading this
address could see clearly that Stalin's new political line deviated
much further from Lenin's plans for the building of socialism than
the political line proposed by Bukharin. But this indirect assault on
Stalin proved largely ineffective.

Stalin and his supporters operated differently. They mobilized
absolutely everything they could against Bukharin. Theoretical differences between Lenin and Bukharin in 1915 and 1916 on the
question of the state were dredged up out of history. So too were

the differences between Lenin and Bukharin at the time of the Treaty of Brest-Litovsk when Bukharin headed the faction of "Left Communists." Quibbling criticism was directed at the writings and speeches of Bukharin during the period 1925–27 when he was arranging the economic and political basis of NEP to conform with the latest circumstances, and militating, along with the whole Party, against "leftist" tendencies. At that time the Party had been exploring an unknown path and it was natural enough that Bukharin should have allowed into his work some inaccurate or ill-considered schemes. It is equally true that there had been quite a lot of mistaken or ill-considered schemes even in Lenin's work during the period 1918–20. Lenin subsequently acknowledged these errors quite openly and mentioned the inevitability of various mistakes occurring in the future. By and large the line taken by Bukharin in 1925–27 was not only correct, it was also the official line of the Party leadership of the day.

There was a particularly crude distortion of Bukharin's comments in 1925–26 on the role of the kulaks and of the capitalist elements in the town and the country, and his slogan "Make yourselves rich!" so soon to be expunged and corrected by Bukharin himself. Bukharin had indeed given much consideration to the fate of the capitalist elements in town and country during the development of NEP. In complete accordance with the views of Lenin, Bukharin spoke then in favour of retaining an individually farmed peasant economy, of developing the initial stages of cooperation which would gradually persuade the peasants toward general cooperative production, and toward socialism itself. Bukharin saw this transition as a prolonged process rather than as a transient revolution; Lenin himself had indicated time and again that the the transition of the peasantry toward socialism would require an entire epoch of history, and that at the same time kulak holdings would continue to develop. Bukharin realized this, without considering it dangerous. The evolution of the kulak class, Bukharin predicted, would move gradually along the lines of state capitalism, since with the development of socialist industry, accompanied by a system of credit-financing by the state, and along with the increase in cooperatively organized work, the kulaks would inevitably be deprived of all possibilities for independent, individualized development. It is also true that Bukharin spoke of the "incorporation of kulak holdings" within the system of the socialist economy. Yet he spoke also of the "alien nature" of the kulak elements in the expanding system of the socialist economy and of the consequent possibility of limiting and reeducating both town and country kulaks even as they competed with socialist elements. He was confident that socialism would always assume the dominating position in every sphere of economic and political life. It goes without saying that this was no more than a precautionary theory—after all, the likelihood was for a rather protracted period of development of the socialist economy along NEP lines.

Bukharin's basic attitude toward this issue was set out in his book *The Road to Socialism and the Union of Workers and Peasants,* published in 1925, which remains his major work on the theory of NEP. The author himself points out in the introduction to this book that the ideas expounded in it were inspired by a long series of conversations with Lenin at the end of 1922. It was essentially this book which provided the theoretical starting-point for the formulation of the "general Party line" in the period 1925–27.

Nevertheless, in the winter and spring of early 1929 much of Bukharin's written and spoken work of the mid-1920s was subjected to a tendentious and unscrupulous reappraisal. Individual words and phrases were lifted from it and often distorted. Bukharin came to be presented as a permanent enemy and opponent of Lenin; an enemy of collectivization and industrialization; an ideological mainstay of the kulak class and all the Nepman profiteering elements throughout the USSR; a channel of Social Democratic influence upon the Bolsheviks; a man whose proposals would lead deliberately to the restoration of capitalism in the USSR. With no reference to sources the assault upon Bukharin and his group had recourse to the same arguments used only a few years previously by the "leftist" opposition against Stalin himself.

Naturally enough, Bukharin defended himself against this onslaught from the massed ranks of the Party machine. He referred not only to the opinions and utterances of Lenin, but to resolutions taken at the Fifteenth Party Congress—the latest one—when victory over "leftist" deviation had been consolidated. These resolutions oriented the Party toward the development and perfecting of NEP policies; the congress had clearly and unambiguously condemned "leftist" calls for some kind of "new revolution" in the countryside directed against the kulaks and Nepman profiteers. Both in theory and in practical formulation the proposals and utterances made by Bukharin were without doubt nearer to what might be called "latter-day Leninism." They were also preferable from the standpoint of allowing the evolution of socialism to occur in an effective, wholesome manner. Nevertheless, in the spring of 1929 Stalin enjoyed a clear majority on the Central Committee of the Party and this decided the outcome of the struggle in his favor. This was amply demonstrated by the next plenary session of the Central Committee held in April of that year.

The April session confirmed Stalin's victory. "Rightist" deviation was condemned and the propagation of opinion and theory described by Stalin as "rightist" was branded as incompatible with Party membership. Bukharin's speech and the addresses made by Rykov and Tomsky were never published; it was further decided to omit more than thirty pages from the published text of Stalin's address, ostensibly in the interests of Party unity. Bukharin disagreed with the resolutions taken at the April session. He could not, of course, have foreseen just where Stalin's policy would eventually lead the Party and the country. However, he recognized the impossibility under present circumstances of waging war openly against a majority of the Central Committee as, in their day, Trotsky, Zinoviev, and Kamenev had done. Difficult times were upon them and Bukharin regarded the preservation of Party unity as essential.

What was clear was that Stalin was taking on the affluent peasantry, who in turn could count on the support of the majority of middle peasants, and that it would be a fight to the death. The battle was fraught with danger and Stalin set about feverishly swelling the ranks of his supporters with the "leftist" opposition members of yesterday. The question of choice arose for Bukharin and he chose, as he thought, the Party, which, even if it were to start carrying out wrong policies, nevertheless remained *his* party. Then at the plenary session of the Central Committee held in November 1929 Rykov read out a written declaration in his own name and those of Bukharin and Tomsky. In this it was stated that the "group of three" stood unconditionally for the general Party line, differing from the majority of the Central Committee only on some matters of detail in its practical application. The "group of three" went on to say in their document that "through the general line, as applied practically in methods approved by the Party, substantial positive achievements had been made overall." For this reason Bukharin, Rykov, and Tomsky announced that their differences with the majority of the Central Committee "were being withdrawn."[3]

This letter, together with the resolutions passed at the November session, untied Stalin's hands once and for all. As early as the end of 1927 Stalin had begun to carry out a policy of extraordinary measures without the approval of the Central Committee and in the teeth of decisions taken at the very recent Fifteenth Party Congress. Now he elected to pursue this method further—to present the Party with a fait accompli, and thus deprive it of the possibility of any alternative decision. At the end of December Stalin suddenly announced the policy of liquidation of the kulaks as a class despite the fact that at the recently held plenary session no decision in that direction had ever been taken. Retreat was by now becoming virtually impossible and, with that clearly in mind, Bukharin, Tomsky, and Rykov decided to approach Stalin in the early hours of New Year's Day to arrive at a reconciliation in personal as well as political terms.

Until recently they had been, as it were, not just comrades-in-arms but actual friends. They used the familiar, second-person singular, form of address and it was Bukharin's standard practice to refer to Stalin not by his forename but by his Party nickname "Koba." Stalin, Voroshilov, and the other members of the Politburo had made a clear demonstration of their friendly attitude to Bukharin. Bukharin was a man knowledgeable in many spheres of activity; during his years of exile he had spent some time in virtually

every major Western country and was a multilinguist. He was extremely well versed in Marx's theory of economics and was to a
slightly lesser extent familiar with Marxist philosophy. There is no
doubt that Lenin was right when he wrote in his *Testament* that
there was something scholastic in Bukharin and his opinions—
Lenin himself probably never even made a serious study of dialectics. Since that time Bukharin had read a number of books on philosophy, and a certain tendency toward schematism and abstruse academic theorizing remained with him. He was teased about this by
some of his friends, and the poet Demyan Bedny once wrote the following verses on the subject which contain more humor than poetic
talent:

> I called on Bukharin, and regret
> He brought me out in a muck-sweat.
> He stunned me with one of his savage looks
> And then snarled, "You're in my bad books.
> You haven't reached the right deduction
> Concerning democracy practiced in production.
>
> I know Lenin didn't see it either,
> But this is how it is decided:
> By achieving solidarity in the negative *"apportium"*
> Of my new buffer-based conception
> As described on the cover of *The ABC of Communism,*
> Allowing for problematic contingencies as well."
> At which point I ran like hell.

Although these lines were penned as early as 1921, during the
period of discussing the role of the trade unions, Bedny included
them in his *Collected Works* which appeared in the mid-1920s.[4]
Bukharin never took offense at this kind of criticism. He was a true
devotee of passionate debating. Before the Revolution he had
argued a good deal with Lenin about the role of the state and the
rights of nations to self-determination. He it was who, in January
and February 1918, disputed Lenin's proposals concerning the
Treaty of Brest-Litovsk and became the founder of the "Left Communist" group that began to issue its own journal. These arguments,
for all their causticity, were conducted without lasting detriment to
the relationships between those involved. At any rate Lenin con-

tinued after 1918 to treat Bukharin with warm affection.

What was not possible was to argue with Stalin and still maintain friendly relations. All friendliness immediately dropped away from Stalin like a mask; he would become not merely rough, but contemptuously and offensively crude, which hurt the easily wounded Bukharin, ever-sensitive to other people. During the April plenary session when Bukharin protested against the acerbic epithets and evaluations being made by Stalin he tried to remind the latter of their friendship, but Stalin replied by continuing in the same insulting tone:

> Bukharin has mentioned personal correspondence with me. He has read out a few letters that show that although we were personal friends yesterday we now differ from each other in our policies. The speeches by Uglanov and Tomsky have sung the same song. It comes down to this, you might say: Old Bolsheviks we are, and suddenly we've fallen out, and we have no respect for each other. I think all this wailing and moaning isn't worth a brass farthing.[5]

Yet, overcoming their grievances, Bukharin, Tomsky, and Rykov went to Stalin in the early hours of New Year's Day hoping to smooth out their personal relationships. Stalin was pleased, of course, and invited them to sit down at the table. Even then, however, Stalin's attitude was one of calculation. Bukharin still retained great popularity within the Party. Rykov was still a member of the Politburo (Bukharin had been expelled from it at the end of 1929) and, more than that, he was chairman of the Council of People's Commissars. Stalin may have emerged victorious from the infighting within the Central Committee but the country and the Party were only just beginning to move further "to the left" down the path earmarked by himself, and he could not be sure how his "revolution from above" would turn out. Bukharin's abilities might yet come in handy.

Early in 1930 Bukharin, who had been excluded from working in the Politburo and the Comintern and also removed from his post as editor-in-chief of *Pravda*, was appointed head of research planning in the USSR All-Union Council of National Economy. This work placed him out of the mainstream of urgent political events as they developed in the country. Yet these very events in many respects were confirming Bukharin's worst fears. All-out mass collectivization, the mass destruction of the kulaks, the use of violence not only toward the kulak, but toward the middle peasant as well and even toward the poor peasant—all of this created an atmosphere of near-crisis in the countryside, reminiscent of the crisis of 1920. Stalin's article "Dizzy from Success," which placed all the blame for the mistakes and shortcomings of all-out collectivization upon local workers, had done something to clear the air. Now, however, an equally all-out movement of the peasants was beginning; they wanted to abandon the collective farms. During the winter of 1929–30 this resulted in the slaughter of more than half of all the cattle, including the horses which provided the main source of haulage in the countryside. National agricultural production for 1930 was significantly below that of 1929 and continued to fall. The grip on the peasantry tightened again at the end of 1930 and once more they were compelled to join collective farms; the pace set for liquidating the kulaks was also stepped up. Numbers of collective farms increased, numbers of displaced kulak families also increased (as did those of the families belong to "kulak collaborators"), while the agricultural output went on declining.

Alarm signals from the countryside were being received in Moscow. Bukharin must have been informed of them, if only by younger disciples and supporters. Nevertheless, the gravest consequences of Stalin's new course were not reported in full in the first six months of 1930. Even worse news was in store for Bukharin. In late 1929 he had acknowledged the mistaken nature of his own "deviation" but he had no wish to associate himself with the active implementation of Stalin's new policy, though this was demanded of recent converts from "rightist deviation" as proof of the sincerity of their declarations. And so Bukharin kept his own counsel and withdrew into himself. He made no more speeches in the various auditoriums. He applied himself assiduously to his work in the research planning section. He virtually stopped seeing Rykov, who still remained a member of the Politburo and had retained his post as chairman of the Council of People's Commissars. He only rarely met with Tomsky. Tomsky had also survived as a Politburo member, though at the end of 1929 he had been sacked from his position as chairman of the All-Union Central Trade-Union Council, which meant he was no longer a leader of the Soviet trade-union movement.

In his recollections of Mayakovsky, Vasili Katanyan gives a descriptive sketch of Bukharin as he appeared in the spring of 1930. (Bukharin was a great admirer of Mayakovsky, the poet of the Revolution though he scarcely knew him personally and in fact did not even know his work all that well). He writes as follows:

If we are to set out all the facts in their chronological order we must begin at the very beginning—Bukharin, as editor of *Pravda*, showed Lenin a poem which had appeared in *Izvestiya* under the title "Life in our times: Constantly in Conference." This noteworthy detail was told to me by Osip Brik and B. F. Malkin. Mayakovsky himself knew about it, of course.

When did Mayakovsky get to know Bukharin? He didn't work for *Pravda* and he had few points of contact with Bukharin's political and social activities. I know of only one conversation between Bukharin and Mayakovsky (told to me by the latter). It was shortly after *Pravda* had published Bukharin's "Nasty Notes" (January 1927). LEF supporters agreed with the basic arguments of Bukharin's statement but went much further in their criticism of Yeseninism. In the course of conversation, with Mayakovsky laying into the younger poets who wrote nothing but little lyrical verses, Bukharin stopped him in a conciliatory manner:

"Well, what do you expect from them, Vladimir Vladimirovich? It's just that youngsters do have . . . their balls."

"Yes, of course," Mayakovsky agreed. "It's O.K.—so long as they're not bigger than their heads."

One other meeting seems to have occurred at the end of December 1927 or in January 1928. We know of it from a letter written by Bukharin which has been preserved among Mayakovsky's papers. It is addressed to Maria Ulyanova, Lenin's sister and permanent deputy to the editor-in-chief of *Pravda*:

Dear Maria,

I can't help thinking that Mayakovsky ought to work for *Pravda*. Please negotiate with him and don't worry about his size or his voice or other equivalent features. He's not so intimidating a person as he seems. Do please negotiate with him.

Yours,

N. Bukharin

P.S. Don't run away with the idea that Mayakovsky has violated, terrorized or otherwise compelled me to give you a letter or anything like that. I write of my own free will, in sound mind and of good judgment.
N.B.[6]

The letter was never sent. Mayakovsky, who was meant to deliver it, left it behind at home. Still, one way or another, his poems did start to appear in *Pravda* from time to time. At any rate six of them were published by that newspaper in 1928. That is not many considering that Mayakovsky wrote more than one hundred twenty poems that year. However, in the following year, 1929, with Bukharin no longer the editor, *Pravda* published only one poem by Mayakovsky.

Mayakovsky's sudden suicide was a grievous blow to Bukharin, as Katanyan recalls:

On the morning of 15 April the coffin with Mayakovsky's body stood in the Conference Hall of the Writers' Club resting on tables pushed together. In the hall, armchairs were being removed, hammers were banging, a dais was being constructed; the artists Tetlin, Levin, and Denisovsky were putting up a large black canopy under which Mayakovsky was to lie. . . . An enormous crowd had filled the courtyard of the club and was growing continuously outside the gates.

Bukharin arrived at the club at midday and could scarcely get through to the door. He was escorted to one of the distant rooms to take his coat off. Then he walked into the Conference Hall and stood there for a long time in front of the coffin.

What was he thinking about? What words were forming in his mind? . . .

"How strange it is, and how painful, to see this large, strong, angular man, this irrepressible rebel, the incarnation of dynamism, lying peacefully with his lips closed on his death-bed. Come on now, let's have you up, Vladimir Vladimirovich! You can't have finished all that thundering! Come on, the joke's over! . . .

"But, alas, it was no joke. It was a tragedy. The great poetic tribune of the Revolution has thundered his last and fallen silent. For ever and ever. . . ." (Taken from N. Bukharin, *Etyudy*, p. 192).

I stood to one side and strove to recall what Mayakovsky had written about Bukharin—it was in a poem on the Sixth Congress of the Comintern in summer the year before last. . . .

Comrade Bukharin
            under the tatty palm fronds
says, "You have lost someone . . ."
And the hall echoes back:
                    You've fallen, a victim . . .
You've fallen, a victim in the fatal struggle.

Here there are no tatty palm fronds but how terribly those words ring today—"You have lost someone."

". . . He undervalued the Raphaels and Pushkins of this world. Yet he had an organic kinship with his age; history itself *roared out* through him at her still surviving forces of conservatism. . . . This death is full of paradox. It is scandalously absurd. It is outrageously tragic. Vladimir Vladimirovich, why, oh why did you do it?!" (Bukharin, op. cit., pp. 197–98).

He was then taken away to that same distant room to put his coat on and a little later Boris Kireyev, the director of the club, came up to me and said that Bukharin would not leave. . . . How about asking him to make a speech? Yes, let's do that.

That's how simple-minded we were. Our reasoning was straightforward: "There are people who have been brought here by a barbarous, incomprehensible piece of news. The anguished crowd in the yard, the balcony ready to be spoken from and a speaker, one of the best speakers in the whole Party. Rightist tendencies? What does that matter? No longer editor of *Pravda*? No longer a member of the Politburo? So what?"

Bukharin paced up and down the room, with his scarf stuffed into his cap. He stopped, leveled his steely blue eyes at us and snapped out, "No!"

He put his overcoat on and Kireyev and I took him out the back way through a little door leading straight out to Herzen Street.[7]

Two

The Sixteenth Party Congress

————— ≫》 ≪《 —————

BUKHARIN WAS an exceptionally robust man, who played sports and rarely had a day's illness. However, he found that any difficult psychological experiences tended to be accompanied by physical indisposition. In the spring of 1930 he caught cold and the cold turned into pneumonia. By the summer he was getting better and in June he went down to the Crimea, to the Black Sea, to complete his convalescence.

The Sixteenth Communist Party Congress was fixed for June of that year. As usual before the congress, Party conferences were held in the regions and republics and these were visited by speakers from the Central Committee who reported on Party activities during the period between congress. To this end Tomsky went down to the Transcaucasian region (Armenia, Georgia, and Azerbaidzhan) and Rykov was sent to the Urals. At the Party conferences in those respective regions Tomsky and Rykov were elected as delegates to the forthcoming congress. Nikolai Burkharin received no such assignment and was thus not elected as a congress delegate. He did, of course, have the right to attend as a member of the Central Committee. His health, however, was not fully restored and he made up his mind to stay away. He sent no letters or declarations to the congress. This was taken by many delegates to be a form of demonstration. P. Postyshev, for example, made the following speech:

Comrade Bukharin has so far said nothing and, as you can see, we do not see him here at congress. His silence is a way of maintaining support for his theory of "organized capitalism," and for his allies, such as the Lovestone group in America. He says nothing, and thus maintains support also for those allies of his within this country who aim to revise our economy.[1]

I. Vareykis also found it necessary to remark upon Bukharin's absence:

It is . . . no accident that Comrade Bukharin is absent from this congress. They say he's on holiday; they say he's not very well. I'm no doctor—perhaps he really is ill. But when every allowance has been made, his conduct cannot possibly be justified. Comrades, we know full well what Lenin's attitude was to congresses. Can it be said that Bukharin's attitude is at all like Lenin's? Is that how Lenin taught us to treat Party congresses?[2]

Another person who condemned Bukharin's silence in strong language was S. M. Kirov:

Comrade Bukharin is absent from the congress. They say he's ill. That must be so. But what follows from that? It follows that Bukharin, only yesterday one of the leaders of the Central Committee, could surely have done something, have found some way to add his voice, to communicate his opinions on the fundamental problems of Party policy. . . . Could not Comrade Bukharin have answered . . . some questions? Could he not at least have set out his ideas in an article?[3]

G. I. Petrovsky condemned Bukharin's behaviour in the sharpest terms:

Particular attention must be paid to Comrade Bukharin. He has been, after all, an ideological supporter of rightist deviation, indeed its chief theorist; he has stirred up opportunism not only inside the All-Union Communist party but also on the scale of the Comintern. One might have expected Comrade Bukharin, just before the Sixteenth Party Congress, to have announced some reaction to all those events that have occurred within the Party and in the Comintern—but no, he says nothing. He did write a good pamphlet against Pope Pius, but we might remind Comrade Bukharin that he has also written another one against the Party. Is it not true that his "Notes of an Economist" represent a pamphlet directed against the plans for the building of socialism? Is it not true that his celebrated speech on the fifth anniversary of Lenin's death was a pamphlet directed against the Party, against its whole organization? . . . Is it not true that life has shattered all that he has built up, all his arguments leveled against the Party? Comrade

Bukharin is silent; he is ill. But Comrade Vareykis was correct when he indicated that Lenin was more seriously ill but he still gave his all to the Party and especially to its congresses. . . . Why should Comrade Bukharin, who made so many mistakes while he was leader of the Comintern, not speak out now, not raise his voice? But no, Comrade Bukharin says nothing; his followers say nothing . . . the fact that he says nothing does not correspond to the spirit of Bolshevism, it is of no use, it is not in the Bolshevik tradition.[4]

Bukharin could have sent some letter or statement to the congress; his silence was not only the result of illness. In November 1929 he had admitted that his own line of policy and his own proposals were in error. But in the summer of 1930 the country's situation was not all that different from what it was in November 1929. Bukharin had been the theorist and ideological proponent of "rightist" deviation, or, to be accurate, of NEP; and he, more than anyone else, had doubted the propriety of liquidating the kulaks and the rates of collectivization laid down in January 1930 by a resolution of the Central Committee. He was incapable of fully retracting his views on NEP and the mutual relations existing between the urban working class and the peasantry. Consequently, he could not express full agreement with the new Stalinist policy which included so many of the ideas appropriated from the theoretical program formulated by the ideological proponents of "leftist" opposition.

However, those colleagues of Bukharin's who had until recently shared his political views, Tomsky, Rykov, and Uglanov, were present at the congress and they could not keep silent. It must be borne in mind that the Sixteenth Party Congress was taking place at a time when it was not yet possible for the Party to draw up a balance sheet of the new political and economic policies. The country was in ferment and the "revolution from above" had only just begun. It was too soon to report back with any decisive success stories. Besides that, the position in the countryside was too dramatic, and no one could predict how the year 1930 would end even as far as agricultural output was concerned. Thus the main "victory" which Stalin was able to celebrate at the Sixteenth Congress was his triumph within the Party over "rightist" deviation. Thus it was that the behaviour and pronouncements of Rykov, Bukharin, and Tomsky came to be the main theme of virtually all the speeches and announcements at that congress rather than the actual problems of economic and political reality.

Uglanov was the first of the "ex-rightists" to speak. His address was a failure in almost all respects, and it was continually interrupted by congress delegates who kept shouting out offensive responses. Tomsky and Rykov were much more experienced in the ways of politics and public speaking. Sensing the mood of the delegates they roundly condemned their own "rightist" opinions and equally decisively expressed support for the "general Party line." They also managed a skillful and convincing defence against many other unjust accusations, like the charge that they had conspired against the Party and had set up their own faction, etc. They expressed their views within the framework of the Central Committee and the Politburo without infringing Party regulations. Tomsky pointed out with ample justification that Party members who had made a mistake at some time in the past should not be required continually to express repentance before the Party:

> Would it be proper if, following a great political struggle, and one which was of international significance, I were to come out on to this platform in order to demonstrate repentance? For a Bolshevik it would be improper. The very term "repentance" is not one of ours, it belongs to the Church.[5]

These words met with the delegates' approval. As for Rykov, he strongly challenged the demand from a number of delegates for him to subject Bukharin to a stinging critical attack. He spoke as follows:

> Bukharin's ideas were wrong and I shall combat them. But tell me what is wrong *now* in Bukharin? We have renounced our mistakes, all of us together. I cannot see why I should curse Bukharin, and not myself for my own mistakes. After all I made the mistakes along with him. Concerning my differences with the Central Committee before the November plenary session it is now proposed that I point the finger at Bukharin and shout, "There he is, stop thief!" For what I have done, for those mistakes which I have committed, I take full responsibility, and I shall not use any Bukharin to

get myself out of a mess. This cannot be demanded of me. For any mistakes made by me *I* must be punished, not Bukharin.[6]

The close attention paid by congress to the speeches of Tomsky and Rykov clearly worried Stalin. The next person to address the meeting after Rykov was Sergei Kirov, one of the finest public speakers in the Party. Unfortunately, his speech at the Sixteenth Congress was more than just skillful, it went to the extremes of demagogic oratory. He roundly condemned the addresses made by Rykov and Tomsky as inadequate and mealymouthed. What was it that Kirov and all the other speakers required of the leaders of "rightist" deviation? They wanted more than an admission that they were wrong and that the Party was correct. They *did* demand repentance from Rykov, Tomsky, and their supporters; they demanded not just an admission of error but a further admission that these mistakes and the whole Bukharin line would deliberately lead to a restoration of capitalism in the USSR. They demanded that Rykov and Tomsky (and also Bukharin and his supporters) should admit that they had in fact been agents of the kulaks within the Party, agents of the bourgeoisie itself. They demanded that the recent "rightists" should admit that to all intents and purposes "rightist" deviation bordered not upon "leftist" deviation, but on out-and-out counterrevolution. Kirov lectured Tomsky and Rykov as follows:

What you should have said is this: that if the right wing of the Party had won the day then eventually the line of right-wing opportunism would have led to the restoration of capitalism.[7]

He continued in this exclamatory manner:

Comrades and leaders of the rightist opposition, as Bolsheviks you must qualify your program and, without going into abstruse theorizing, you must state directly that that program is essentially a kulak program the fulfillment of which would eventually bring down the dictatorship of the proletariat and lead to the restoration of capitalism![8]

But neither Rykov, Tomsky, nor Bukharin could say all of that. It was their belief (and although they had admitted mistakes they had not changed their views completely) that they had been defending Lenin's NEP program, Lenin's program of conciliation, Lenin's plan for the building of socialism. They had long since grown accustomed to hearing accusations like those made by Kirov—Trotsky and Zinovyev had made them in regard to the whole Party policy in the period 1925–27. It now transpired one way or another that virtually every speaker after Kirov paid most of his attention not to current problems concerned with the building of socialism, not even to the history of the Party struggle against "rightist deviation," but to "exposing" what Rykov, Tomsky, and Uglanov had said in their congress speeches. Take, for example, the leader of the Ukrainian delegation, S. Kosior, who touched lightly upon things in the Ukraine (which were anything but good) and then went on directly to say, "Comrades, I wish to devote most of the time allowed for my speech to the addresses made earlier by those of the right."[9] The congress now had assumed such a mood that a businesslike address made by Nadezhda Krupskaya on the subject of culture and education was constantly interrupted by cries from the floor, "Speak about Bukharin, say something about Rykov and Tomsky's speeches!" "Talk about Tomsky and Rykov!" "Not enough. Be more precise!" "Not clear enough!" "Unsatisfactory in the extreme!" "Speak about Tomsky and Rykov!" etc. Krupskaya answered the hecklers with the words, "Be patient. Please listen to what I have to say about that other front which is now of the utmost significance and to ignore which could only be described as rightist deviation!"[10] This caused laughter among the delegates and for a while the heckling died down.

That day, the Sixteenth Communist Party Congress passed the following resolution:

Congress draws the attention of the whole Party to the fact that opportunists of every complexion, but especially those of the right, have adopted another maneuver which amounts to a formal acknowledgment of earlier mistakes and formal agreement with the general Party line without backing up this acknowledgment by working and fighting to promote the general line, all of which betokens in actual fact a sidestep from open conflict with the Party into hidden conflict or the awaiting of a propitious moment to renew the attack on the Party.

The Party is obliged to wage war in the most ruthless manner against this kind of double-dealing and deceit, and to demand from those who admit mistakes that they demonstrate the sincerity of their admissions by active support for the general Party line. Failure to respond to this demand will necessarily incur the most severe official reprisals.

Congress affirms that the views of the rightist opposition are incompatible with membership of the Communist party.[11]

Meetings of the Sixteenth Party Congress continued for more than two weeks. On the morning of 13 July Zatonsky announced the results of the elections to the Central Committee of the Communist party. The composition of the new Central Committee differed very little from the one elected three years before at the Fifteenth Congress. Bukharin, Rykov, and Tomsky had been reelected despite the volume of criticism directed at them. Of the former "leftists" Georgi Piatakov was also reelected and he became the first deputy of the People's Commissariat for Heavy Industry. Uglanov was not elected; he had been head of Party organization for five years and head of the People's Commissariat for Labor. Also dismissed from the Central Committee was F. Ugarov, a prominent trade-union activist who was appointed after the congress to a secondary post in industry. An Old Bolshevik, A. Dogadov, accused of taking a "soft line" toward rightist deviation was demoted from the Central Committee to candidate status. Tomsky was sacked from the Politburo. Of the recently turned "rightist" leaders only Rykov remained in the Politburo and he also retained his position as chairman of the Council of People's Commissars. However, in December 1930 the plenary session of the Central Committee removed Rykov from the Politburo and a resolution of the Central Executive Committee relieved him of his duties as head of the Soviet government. Rykov was appointed people's commissar for communications and his place as chairman of the Council of Commissars was taken over by V. M. Molotov. Tomsky was soon to become director of the state publishing house, OGIZ. Bukharin continued as head of the research planning section of the Council of National Economy. Following the reorganization of the leadership and the abolition of that council Bukharin's section was transferred to the Commissariat for Heavy Industry.

Three

Nikolai Bukharin: 1931–33

————— »»«« —————

DIFFICULT though it must have been Bukharin kept out of high-level politics during the period 1931–33 and did not even attempt to get involved. This was not because he had suffered a defeat and seen his economic and political theories declared wrong. It may well be that in these arduous years Bukharin became convinced once and for all that he had been right. But he could change nothing and it was not in his character to take pleasure in downfalls and failures.

The events which occurred at that time in the USSR are now well known. The enforced collectivization of the peasantry went ahead. In all regions of the country tens of thousands of collective farms (*kolkhozy*) were set up, without the machinery, the know-how, and the leadership to run them properly. At the same time hundreds of thousands of kulak families were forcibly transported away to remote regions, as well as hundreds of thousands of families consisting of solid middle-peasant stock who refused to enter the collectives; and large numbers of other peasant families, not excluding the poorest of them, resisted either the establishment of collective farms or the destruction of the churches and thus fell automatically into the category of "kulak-collaborators." Entire villages were uprooted from the Cossack regions and transported to the north. Agricultural output continued to fall, although grain-requisitioning improved. The state continued to export grain in order to boost the foreign currency reserves. Finally this resulted in a severe famine embracing all the grain-producing regions along the Volga, in the North Caucasus, Kazakhstan and Central Asia and, most of all, in the southern regions of the Ukraine where millions of peasants died for lack of food. Even in the cities the situation was not much better. Rationing had been introduced long before this. Now the passport system was reintroduced in order to prevent a mass exodus of the rural population into the cities where it was still just possible to scrape a living for one's family.

A vast industrial building program was carried out on a nationwide scale, with huge plants and factories forming up one after another. Even so the Five-Year Plan was not completed according to the scheduled program despite colossal capital investment and enormous efforts by the whole nation. The perceptible growth which did occur was largely confined to heavy industry. The developments in various branches of light industry envisaged by the Five-Year Plan occurred all too slowly, or not at all. There was a shortage of raw materials for which at that time light industry depended largely on the countryside. For this reason the production of sugar, meat, butter, milk, linen, and leather goods, far from increasing, fell during the five-year period from 1928 to 1932. The output of cottons and woolens marked time. Building for housing was cut back sharply. At the same time the numbers of working-class people doubled in five years rather than rising by one third as envisaged by the plan. This was due largely to the influx of ruined peasants into the cities. Naturally the recently unemployed or those who had been poor peasants perhaps found some satisfaction in their new working lives. However, the standard of living of skilled workers in 1932 and 1933 was much lower than in 1927 and 1928 which, once again, was at variance with the Five-Year Plan.

Nikolai Bukharin was an economist, and he could not fail to see what was happening in his country. Equally he realized that a return to the past was impossible. The reality of the years 1927–28 had passed away and could not be brought back. Some solution must be found to the problems created by the new economic and social circumstances which had arisen.

It goes without saying that a feeling of discontent existed throughout the country in the widest circles and that this found some reflection in the ranks of the Party. In the period 1930–33 a number of quite small oppositional groups sprang up, the majority of them operating like underground conspirators. Among the best known were the Ryutin and Eysmont-Tolmachov groups. Dissatisfaction with the current state of affairs was also expressed by some members of the Central Committee, such as V. Lominadze and S. Syrtsov. It was natural that many of the members of these oppositional groups tried to meet Bukharin in order to get from him some advice or support. Bukharin, however, avoided such encounters. With circumstances as they were he saw no alternative to Stalin's leadership and considered any form of constructive opposition to be out of the question. On the other hand he had no desire to participate in the implementation of Stalin's policy of doing violence to the countryside. Many of Bukharin's recent followers (the "Bukharin school") behaved differently. Some of them threw themselves actively into carrying out Stalin's policies (A. Stetsky, et al.). Others, on the contrary, joined one of the various conspiratorial oppositional groups (D. Maretsky, A. Slepkov, et al.). All of them were ceasing to have any contact with Bukharin.

During these years Bukharin stopped meeting Stalin, though he did continue to see Stalin's wife, Nadezhda Alliluyeva, fairly frequently. Bukharin had been friends with her for a long time, and in her relationships with other people she was far from sharing her husband's opinions and demands. It seems probable that ultimately this became the main reason for her suicide. Bukharin hardly ever encountered any of the members of the Politburo.

Bukharin saw his duties in the scientific planning section as anything but a mere formality. He was quick to familiarize himself with all the circumstances and proceeded not only to formulate a plan for the development of scientific research and scientific institutions during the next five-year period but to begin work in his own section on the very methodology of scientific planning and on the problems of studying science. Apart from the journals *The Science of Production* (for engineers and technicians) and *Science and Technology* (a technical journal for mass circulation) published jointly by the sections for scientific research and for technical propaganda on Bukharin's initiative and with him as editor, in 1931 a new journal began to appear, *Socialist Reconstruction and Science (Sorena)*, intended for skilled personnel in scientific research, technology, and economics. Defining the main aims of this journal Bukharin wrote:

> The present journal has the following aims:
>
> 1) It is to present to the readers innovative articles giving guidance and linking together all scientific and technical work with the tasks laid down by the technical and economic plans of Soviet reconstruction and the general political tasks of the proletariat as defined by directives from the Party and its Central Committee.
>
> 2) It is to present theoretical articles in the most important disciplines, earmarking the main problems of greatest urgency as well as monitoring meticulously the achievements of foreign scientific thinking.
>
> 3) It is to present articles on all the most important problems of technology, nevertheless earmarking the most fundamental and urgent among them and throwing light on all the most important technical achievements.
>
> 4) It is to address itself to the solution of problems of policy in scientific research connected with technology (questions of risk in scientific research, technical assets, etc.).
>
> 5) It is to pose questions concerning the deployment of labor in scientific research and technology (decentralization of scientific and technological institutions, greater proximity to places of production, principles of combination, etc., etc.).
>
> 6) It is to chronicle and present information about both foreign and Soviet science and technology, to throw light on the activity of corresponding institutions, etc., with constant emphasis not on the formal aspects of this activity but on its essential material nature.
>
> 7) It is to present systematic reviews of the achievements of science and technology in solving problems.
>
> 8) It is to organize an appropriate bibliographical section. . . . To live for the business of socialist reconstruction, to work for it and to triumph—this is the ultimate aim of our journal.[1]

The first issue of the journal opened with a philosophical article written by Bukharin himself and entitled "Theory and Practice from the Standpoint of Dialectical Materialism"; this was a new exposition of the paper read at the Second International Congress on the History of Science and Technology held in London.

Bukharin's visit to England, it is interesting to note, was virtually ignored by the Soviet press. It was remarked on by the English press, albeit with some disapproval: one English newspaper wrote that Bukharin had "slipped through England like a snake." In

Moscow the visit was given mention only in the evening paper *Vechernyaya Moskva*. An erstwhile contributor to that newspaper, A. V. Khrabrovitsky, records the following recollection:

In 1931 I was working as a reporter in the editorial office of *Vechernyaya Moskva*. As soon as I learned that Bukharin, then head of the scientific and research section of the All-Union Council of National Economy, had gone to London to attend the Congress on the History of Science and Technology, I began to make inquiries about his return. When he did get back I telephoned him immediately and asked him to write something about his visit for *Vechernyaya Moskva*. The initiative came from me but I acted with the approval of the editorial staff. Bukharin agreed and I asked whether I might collect the manuscript from him at his Kremlin flat. Early one morning I called on him and was given a handwritten article. Efim Tseitlin, Bukharin's assistant, was there too and he admonished me that there could be no question of making any corrections or alterations whatsoever. I went straight from the Kremlin to the printing house where *Vechernyaya Moskva* was run off and I dictated the article to a shorthand-typist. . . .

It was entitled "An Outing in Europe" and that same evening it appeared on the front page. (Researchers should consult the issues for May–June 1931.) The interest aroused by the article was considerable, since no other newspaper was publishing anything like it. Bukharin had descended from the heights and was now in the shadows. He knew it was out of the question to offer his article to anyone himself, so the proposal which came to him from *Vechernyaya Moskva* was most opportune. I remember being given a bonus for my initiative. I was then not quite nineteen and this brief encounter with the celebrated Bukharin was a fascinating experience for a young newspaperman. Bukharin actually was an extremely pleasant, solicitous, and affable man who liked a joke. From then on I tried to attend meetings and occasions at which he was to speak and to write them up for *Vechernyaya Moskva*. My album of cuttings for 1931–32 contains seven notices which relate to Bukharin.

On 31 June 1931 I published a piece describing a visit to Moscow by a delegation of English scientists and, in particular, a banquet in their honor which was attended by Bukharin, Radek, Kerzhentsev, F. N. Petrov, Professor B. M. Zavadsky, Professor B. M. Gessen, and other prominent people. I recall that Bukharin spent the whole evening in conversation (without an interpreter) with the biologist Julian Huxley. When I questioned him afterwards he said, "I could have spoken to the lot of them but I consider it more useful to talk to one person. . . ." Then on 14 August 1931 another of my reports described a meeting in Sokolniki Park with Bukharin speaking on technological propaganda. Part of it ran as follows: "Workers, railwaymen, and students filled the theatre, standing in the gangways, packed like sardines around the rostrum. Crowds of people who had not been able to get in listened outside to an open-air radio broadcast of the meeting." Bukharin's speeches invariably attracted that sort of impassioned attention. Another of my reports (27 August) opened with the words, "The Column Room was full to overflowing. . . ." On further occasion, when Bukharin was one of the speakers describing the London Congress on the History of Science and Technology in the hall of the Communist Academy, people flocked there in such hordes that the building was literally besieged. Despite my official pass and a special note from my editorial office I simply could not force my way through the crush into the building and I had to get in, along with some other people, through a first-floor window. My report (published on 1 September) omitted any mention of "a siege," however, our head of information having told me not to "advertise leaders of the opposition."

When Bukharin addressed large audiences his speeches were, of course, hortatory ones winding up with grand, rousing phrases. Here are one or two typical examples. "Calling upon all the strengths of the working classes we shall storm the fortresses of technology just as we have stormed the fortresses of politics and economics . . . the great battle of the giants will be won. . . ." (*Vechernyaya Moskva*, 14 August 1931) "At the very time when the old world is wallowing in an awareness of its own desperate plight, waiting for the revolutionary Vesuvius to erupt, on we go to a splendid new victory in technological reconstructions!" (27 August) These speeches also contained severe criticism of current shortcomings, though they were characterized by spontaneity, simplicity, and humour. "General laughter" is a phrase which crops up frequently in reports. I recall one meeting between workers and scientists on the shopfloor in the Amo (now Likhachev) factory. Someone from the floor criticized a certain professor of metallurgy, whereupon Bukharin, who was on the panel, put his thumb to his ear and made the usual gesture indicating someone who is slightly off his head. There was once another meeting, in his room at the Council of National Economy, when he referred to the head of Central Park, B. N. Glan, as Madame Glanshy. . . . I know these are minor details but they do seem to me to be typical of this particular man.[2]

Mass meetings were not the only audiences addressed by Bukharin during 1931–32. He was a full member of the Academy of Sciences and indeed a member of its ruling presidium, and in June 1931 he read a substantial paper at an extraordinary session of the academy on the subject, "The Struggle Between the Two Worlds, and the Tasks of Science." In August of that year Bukharin read another paper at a meeting of worker-leaders in scientific research institutions and technical colleges. It was entitled "Socialist Reconstruction and the Fight for Technology" and it concerned technological propaganda and its organization.

The year 1931 saw the first All-Union Conference on the Planning of Scientific Research Work. It was instigated by Bukharin and the paper which he read there was in essence a wide-ranging and exhaustive survey of the problems relating to the planning of scientific work. The State Publishing House for Socioeconomic Materials published this paper in booklet form. In the same year the Red Proletariat Publishing House issued, also in booklet form, another of Bukharin's articles, "On the Propaganda of Technology and Its Organization."

A young economist by the name of E. P. Frolov worked alongside Bukharin from 1929 to 1933 in the research section. Thirty-five years later he wrote in his memoirs:

From the autumn of 1929 until the summer of 1933 I worked as deputy to the head of the scientific research section of the Council of National Economy, Nikolai Ivanovich Bukharin. Our business dealings were not regimented but it transpired that every morning, about a quarter of an hour after he arrived at work, I would drop into his room and for half an hour or forty minutes we would exchange plans concerning what work had to be done and how best to do it. . . . I used to arrive with a single sheet of paper on which I had jotted down the night before a list of topics to be talked over. I marked them off in letters of the Greek alphabet: alpha, beta, gamma, delta, and so on. This form of indexing was often used by Lenin himself and then I first encountered it with Nikolai Bukharin. It's clear that Bukharin borrowed this method from Lenin and, well, I suppose I was copying the pair of them . . . I might add that Bukharin had borrowed a number of Lenin's devices to facilitate reading and writing, such as, for instance, underlining once, twice, or three times individual words or expressions which he wished to bring out, writing exclamation marks, question marks, his initials or the Latin letters "N.B." for *nota bene*, etc. I observed also that Bukharin's handwriting was very similar to Lenin's. . . . In general terms it should be said that there was a great deal of Lenin about Bukharin, both in external appearance (the same build, the same brawny frame, the same reddish coloring, the same huge, clean forehead, similarly modest and straightforward personalities, the same capacity for painstaking hard work!) and in relation to the inner character (an infinite devotion to the affairs of the working class, high principles, courage, a gentleness of spirit, humanitarianism, and a remarkable degree of philanthropy). I noticed the similarities then and I often think back to them now.

Bukharin often insisted that I must go over "little trifles"; he would urge me to go into all the minor details of a certain incident or fact. And all too often I was put to shame. In something which I had considered negligible Bukharin would find the key—and the only key—to the correct solution of a problem. Frequently he would make essential corrections by approaching the problem from a quite different angle from my own, from an angle which, as far as I was concerned, was unknown, novel, and frequently surprising by its suddenness. Conversations with Bukharin were for me a creative school and I realized at that time why it was that young people found him so magnetic. During the conversation I used to jot down his remarks on the same piece of paper which lay before me. Later I would think them over, considering whether he was right or wrong, and I was amazed by the acuity of his thinking.

I remember one conversation . . . I was expounding the various approaches to the Uralo-Kuznetsk problem, criticizing all of them and outlining the directions in which I thought the solution should be sought. Bukharin listened to me very closely, with great concentration and without interrupting. But I got carried away and, summoning up all my powers of cogent persuasion, I began to speak in pathos-laden terms of the true significance of finding a correct solution to the Uralo-Kuznetsk problem for the building of socialism. Then at last Bukharin broke in. "Well, well . . . here you go again about the building of socialism," he said, drawing the words out in a way that was unusual for him and I seemed to see an ironic smile flitting across his face. But he spoke the sentence without irritation, quite calmly, though with reluctance, rather as if he were feeling tired. I confess the meaning of his sentence escaped me for a while and I couldn't think of a reply. I saw that I had somehow plucked a delicate string which had its own painful resonances for him. His words had expressed enormous disappointment and offence.

It came to me later that Bukharin had quite unwittingly opened his soul to me and it was full of arduous and agonizing experiences. I thought to myself, "What's wrong with talking about the building of socialism and why did he lay such emphasis on the word 'again'?" I was puzzled and rather pained by his remark. "I don't understand you. . . . Have I done something criminal? I mean, I was talking about serious things. The way things are with us, anything seems like the building of socialism." "Yevgeniy Petrovich, what do you mean you don't understand? . . . Am I against building socialism? Do I need to be taught how to do it? I thought you and I had sorted that out ages ago. . . . Do you still really believe those lies they surround me with? . . ." He looked down for a moment, bit his lip and scowled. I had no idea what thoughts flashed through his mind in that instant. Then, as often happened with him, he pulled himself together, a

broad smile lit up his face, the mischievous Bukharin glint came into his
eyes and he said, "Anyway, don't you get upset. I've got nothing against
you. Let's say Bukharin made another mistake, this time a tactical one."
And he burst into happy laughter. . . .[3]

It is important to remember that in the early 1930s the problem
of the long-term planning and state control of scientific research,
embracing the whole gamut of the sciences, was a quite unfamiliar
one. Equally unfamiliar was the problem of linking science closely
to production and on a nationwide basis. The USSR was the first to
tackle these problems, along with the whole question of state planning of the national economy. In other countries planning and control of research by the state did not present itself as a problem until
after World War II when the costs incurred by the major powers for
scientific research leaped up, with the problems multiplying by
scores or even hundreds. Unfortunately this came about not because the role of science was seen to be of outstanding importance as
a means of production, but because the development of a wide
range of scientific methods was necessary for creating all types of
modern weaponry, including atomic and hydrogen bombs, rockets,
and chemical as well as bacteriological devices.

At any rate, the last two or three decades have witnessed the
rapid growth of a new branch of knowledge—the study of science—
including subdivisions such as the economics of science, scientific
planning, science and technology, science and production, the social role of science, and so on. In this regard, a number of various
undertakings initiated by Bukharin and his team in Soviet research
planning and a number of ideas introduced as early as the period between 1931 and 1934 in the journal *Sorena* have come to a significant development in the modern study of science in Russia and
abroad.

The work involved in the planning and coordination of science
which Bukharin did for the Council of National Economy increased
his stature and scope within the presidium of the Soviet Academy of
Sciences. This led in turn to a strengthening of business and friendly
relations between Bukharin and many of the leading scientists in the
USSR. For instance, he became closely associated with as promi-

nent a figure as Nikolai Ivanovich Vavilov. In those years Vavilov
was director of the All-Union Institute of Applied Botany and New
Cultures. He organized innumerable expeditions all over the world
and on his initiative new selection stations were established and bio-
logical research took off in new directions. A particularly intimate
friendship grew up between Bukharin and academician Abram Fyo-
dorovich Ioffe, the founder and director of the Leningrad Institute
of Physics and Technology. Bukharin frequently visited Ioffe at
home and became a friend of the whole family.

Another man whom Bukharin met frequently was Ivan Petrovich Pavlov. Relations between the two of them varied from
period to period. In the spring of 1924 Pavlov gave a series of lectures in the Leningrad Military Medical Institute in which he attempted a systematic exposition of twenty-five years' work on the
physiology of the cerebral hemispheres in the brain of a dog. These
lectures were taken down in shorthand since it was Pavlov's inten-
tion to have them published later in book form. The first of them
was devoted, however, not to physiology, but to politics, in the first
instance to a critique of Marxism in general and the Bolsheviks in
particular. Pavlov began by admitting that he rarely left his laboratory and never read the tendentious Soviet press. He constructed
his lecture for the most part upon an analysis of two pamphlets by
Bukharin, *The Proletarian Revolution and Culture* and *The ABC of
Communism*. Pavlov came down heavily on Bolshevik calls for world
revolution; he condemned the Revolution in Russia which had led
the country into civil war and set it back several decades especially
in the realm of economics. According to him the Bolsheviks were
spending more resources on supporting the revolutionary movement in Japan, or some such country, than on the development of
science in their own land. After mentioning the horrors and the
huge cost of the recently ended civil war Pavlov went on to exclaim,
"How can they speak of building and culture, these people—including Bukharin—who are up to their elbows in blood?" He continued
in this vein. "Marxism, or the Communist party . . . is of the pure
kind because they [the Communists] have decided that it represents
the truth. They wish to know nothing else and they sacrifice every-

thing to their one end." Pavlov concluded his lecture by addressing
the following words to his audience:

And if you are going to develop the right attitude to science, if you get a
really solid knowledge of it, then it won't matter whether you're Communists, "rabfak" students, or whatever—you will still admit that Marxism and
communism are far from being the absolute truth; they are a theory, one of
many theories, perhaps containing a partial truth, perhaps not. And
throughout your lives you will watch from the standpoint of freedom, not of
slavery, such as this is.

The shorthand report of this lecture by Pavlov soon came into
Bukharin's hands. He decided upon an immediate reply and in the
course of a few days he wrote one of his most interesting and brilliant articles: "On World Revolution, Our Country, Culture, etc. (A
Reply to Professor Pavlov)." This was published in the journal *Red
Virgin Soil*, volumes 1 and 2, 1924. Naturally it was not difficult for
Bukharin to refute Pavlov's extremely primitive criticism of Marxism, the October Revolution, world revolution, and the international situation. The keenness of the polemical onslaught in his article was tempered by respect for his opponent and with an
emphasis on the outstanding services of Pavlov to physiology and to
science and humanity in general. As Bukharin put it:

The methodological starting points and the results achieved by the research work of Professor Pavlov are weapons in the powerful arsenal of ma-
terialist ideology. And, in this day and age, materialism is by and large the
ideology of the proletariat. . . . For this reason it is easy to understand the
respect which in our Marxist environment is enjoyed (and will continue to
be enjoyed) by any scientist who speaks out bravely against the flood of
vague mysticism. I repeat: such a scientist, whatever his own subjective in-
tentions, is working for the same cause that we revolutionary Marxists are
working for. And Professor Pavlov belongs to the ranks of such scientists.

Some time later Bukharin was introduced to Pavlov, chatted
with him and paid visits to his laboratory. Once he invited Pavlov to
his home and Pavlov accepted. Everyone in the Bukharin family
had an interest in biology and the house contained all sorts of collections, especially ornithological ones including numerous cages with
live birds in them. Bukharin actually kept a fox in the Kremlin and

Svetlana Alliluyeva (Stalin's daughter) in her book *Twenty Letters to a Friend* wrote that this creature, "Bukharin's fox," lived on in the Taynitsky Garden in the Kremlin long after Bukharin himself had ceased to exist. Pavlov was taken aback by how well his host knew his biology and how expertly he found his way through questions which seemed so remote from Marxism. From then on Pavlov and Bukharin enjoyed most respectful and even friendly mutual relations despite the difference in their ages—at the time Bukharin was a little over forty and Pavlov not far short of eighty.

Bukharin's work for the Council of National Economy, the presidium of the Academy of Sciences and the USSR Central Executive Committee did not keep him fully occupied. He continued to contribute to a number of journals and newspapers. In 1930 he published a pamphlet in *Pravda* under the title *Financial Capital in the Gown of the Pope*. In one of the collections of the Council of National Economy he published another article, "Socialist Reconstruction and the Natural Sciences." He took part in the preparation of a volume celebrating the sixtieth birth of D. B. Riazanov and wrote the preface, "Battle Stations." In conjunction with A. Deborin he wrote a short notice "The Teachings of Marx and Their Historical Significance" (Academy of Sciences Publishing House, 1933). In addition to all this he continued the massive task of editing the second and third editions of Lenin's *Complete Works*. Only a few volumes of this collection were issued under the editorship of L. B. Kamenev; Bukharin was the editor of most of them, along with V. Molotov and M. Saveliev. (A few volumes were also edited partly by V. Adoratsky and I. Skvortsov-Stepanov, though the latter died in 1928). Bukharin devoted some considerable time to literature as well, especially poetry. At a meeting of the Academy of Sciences in 1931 called to mark the seventy-fifth anniversary of Heinrich Heine's death it was Bukharin who read the main tribute, a paper entitled "Heine and Communism." A year later the country marked the centenary of the death of that other great German poet, Goethe. At the anniversary conference on this occasion Bukharin read a major tribute, a paper called, "Goethe and His Historical Significance."

The name of Bukharin appeared from time to time, though not

all that frequently, in the pages of the central press during the years 1931–33. In the first place the many calls for increasing the tempo of socialist construction were commonly accompanied not only by outbursts directed against "counterrevolutionary Trotskyism" but by similar ones against "right-wing opportunism." For example, in *Pravda*'s leading article on 1 January 1931 there was the following comment:

> . . . the rightists have tried consistently to wreck this socialist offensive by speaking out against industrialization, against collectivization, against the liquidation of the kulak class, and by striving in practice for a restoration of capitalism.

And, although *Pravda* gives no indication of who exactly these "rightists" were, everyone knew that Bukharin, Rykov, and Tomsky were the ones first concerned. Theoretical articles in *Pravda, Izvestiya, Bolshevik*, and other papers made frequent mention of mistakes made by Bukharin in 1918 ("Left Communism"), his "semianarchic" mistakes on the issue of the state (1916) and his "theory of equilibrium," not to mention his theory of "kulak incorporation into socialism."

The year 1932 saw *Pravda*'s thirtieth birthday, and naturally the edition of 5 May was devoted in its entirety to this anniversary. Nevertheless, neither this issue nor the one for the following day made the slightest reference to the name of Bukharin, who had been the paper's editor-in-chief for almost twelve years. On the contrary, the leading article read as follows:

> Opportunists have understood the function of *Pravda*, the significance of the authority which this newspaper has acquired under Party control. They have attempted to use this authority against the Party but received a decisive rebuff. That is what happened in the first period of the fight against Trotskyism in 1923. That is what happened in the first months of the fight against Bukharinite opposition, a time when right-wing opportunists were entrenched in the *Pravda* organization.

When Bukharin's name cropped up on the pages of *Pravda*, however, it was by no means always accompanied by the epithet "right-wing opportunist." For instance, on publication of the papers of the Sixth Congress of Soviets it was announced that the following members had been elected to the new Council of the Central Executive Committee of the USSR: N. I. Bukharin, A. Rykov, and M. Tomsky. On 6 August 1931 *Pravda* published a substantial report written by Bukharin for the Party Central Committee, "On Technological Propaganda and Its Organization." A few days later the paper devoted a special leader to the problems of technological propaganda from which it is clear that the Central Committee passed a resolution based on Bukharin's report and intended to improve the whole situation with regard to technological propaganda. In the same month a group of scientists, including Bukharin, announced through the columns of *Pravda* that the Academy of Sciences was extending its involvement in the training of skilled scientists in the country and setting up new postgraduate courses. Examples are given of the active participation of leading institutions of the Academy of Sciences in the building of socialism.

In January and February 1932 the Seventeenth Party Conference was held. Bukharin spoke in the debate concerning a report made by S. Ordzhonikidze. His report had been published in *Pravda* on 3 February under the headline, "Scientific Research in the Service of Socialism." Then in October of that year *Pravda* published a long article by Bukharin, "The New Humanity," devoted to the fortieth anniversary of Gorky's debut in literary and social affairs. And on 15 December the newspaper printed a long speech by Bukharin at the Fifth All-Union Congress of Engineering and Technological Workers: "The World Crisis, the USSR and Technology."

Earlier, in 1930, clearly on the initiative of Bukharin, an interesting document of Lenin's had been published, "Lenin's Observations On Bukharin's Book *The Economics of the Transition Period*." This had first seen the light of day in issue No. 11 of *Lenin's Collection*. These collections had started coming out as early as 1924 and they were prepared for press in tandem with the *Collected Works of Lenin* arranged by the Party Central Committee Lenin Institute. It was envisaged that the collections would publish, on a fairly modest scale, notes and letters written by Lenin but never published in his lifetime and in most cases never intended for publication. Between 1924 and 1929 a total of ten collections had been published. In 1931 the Soviet Economics Publishing House (*Sotsekgiz*) printed Lenin's observations on Bukharin's book in pamphlet form. According to the normal practice when publishing Lenin's notes in such form it was seen as proper to include not only Lenin's actual notes but also those sentences, paragraphs, and in some cases whole pages from Bukharin's text on which Lenin had written sometimes the briefest note or where Lenin had merely underlined a word or two or a couple of lines here and there.

Bukharin's book, *The Economics of the Transition Period*, is known to have been written in the spring of 1920 and published in May of that year. In it he proposed to set out a full scheme and even create an economic and political theory dealing with the transition from capitalism to socialism based largely on the experience of Soviet Russia. The book was planned to consist of two parts, but only Part One, *A General Theory of the Process of Transformation*, actually appeared in print. Part Two never saw the light of day since by the spring of 1921 not only had political and economic circumstances changed but so had all the fundamental ideas of the Bolsheviks on the economics and politics of the transitional period.

In other words, Bukharin had constructed all his theories and conclusions on that set of circumstances which later came to be known as "war communism." He had looked upon this "war communism" not as a temporary state born of the exceptional circumstances of the civil war and the series of economic mistakes committed by the Bolsheviks, but as a normality, as the only possible transitional period from capitalism to socialism. No one in the Party, and that includes Bukharin, foresaw the introduction of NEP which turned out to be the only sensible and in the circumstances the only possible transitional economic policy. Thus it was that Bukharin's book rapidly became obsolete and mistaken and it was never republished.

It is clear from Lenin's comments in the margins of this book that he read it not only with great interest but also with complete understanding and approval. Although Lenin had certainly objected to a number of Bukharin's observations, usually because of their obscurity or excessive complexity, on the whole he welcomed the publishing of the book. Here and there in the margins one often comes across exclamations such as "good," "very good," "important," "quite true," and so on. The least successful chapter from the

NEP point of view was, of course, chapter 10, "Extra-Economic Compulsion in the Transitional Period," but even this one received Lenin's wholehearted approval. To give an example, Bukharin writes in this chapter: "Large numbers of the middle, and even to some extent of the poor, peasantry constantly vacillate, moved at one time by hatred of the capitalists and landowners because of their exploitation of others, a hatred which impels them toward communism and, at another, by the feelings of a property owner (and therefore, in times of famine, a speculator) which impel them into reactionary attitudes. This latter finds expression in resistance to the state monopoly of grain; in an impulse toward free trading, which is nothing less than speculation, and in speculation, which is nothing less than free trading; in opposition to the system of labour conscription and to all general forms of state control over economic anarchy . . ." The underlining was done by Lenin and opposite that sentence he has written "Quite true."

Further on Bukharin writes: "Taking the broad view, proletarian compulsion in all its forms, from executions to labor conscription, however paradoxical this might sound, amounts to the manufacturing of Communist man out of human material of the capitalist age. . . ." The last part of the sentence was underlined by Lenin and marked by three lines in the margin against which he has written "exactly!" At the end of the tenth chapter Lenin has put, "This chapter is excellent!" and in conclusion he gives a general appraisal of Bukharin's book which is extremely favorable. Parodying the excessively complex language of its theoretical chapters, he wrote:

The excellent qualities of this excellent book suffer some disqualification in so far as they are limited by these circumstances: that, firstly, the author fails to consolidate his postulates upon solid, though brief factual material, whereas in literary terms he has it in plenty. Greater factual consolidation would have freed this book from the defects in its "sociological," or rather philosophical character. . . . Secondly, the author is not concrete enough in his analysis of economic questions, often having recourse to what are called "technological terms" (*Termintechnicus*) or "conceptual scholasticism" (*Begriffscholastic*) and failing to realize that many unhappy terms and formulations are enradicated in philosophy. . . . One may be permitted to express the hope that this minimal drawback will disappear from the future editions which are so essential for our reading public and will bring further honor

upon our Academy, an Academy which we now congratulate with the splendid achievement of one of its members. 31 May 1920

One wonders just why this work was published and especially in
separate pamphlet form. It goes without saying that Bukharin was
not trying to show yet again how highly Lenin had esteemed him
and praised one of his books. After all, the whole of Lenin's praise
relates to things that were wrong, under the circumstances of NEP.
It is possible that, well aware of Stalin's penchant for collecting mistakes made by his opponents, Bukharin wished to demonstrate that
in this instance he had been wrong in good company, with Lenin
and the whole Party and that not every mistake is a manifestation of
some kind of hostile class-conscious deviation. But what is more
probable is that Bukharin wished to express an indirect protest
against the revival of the policy of "war communism" in connection
with the new "third revolution" in the countryside. He seems to
have been saying, "All this love of compulsion has been got over
long, long ago: socialism in the countryside cannot be constructed
by using methods of extra-economic compulsion—otherwise it will
all end as badly as it did in the spring of 1921." It is curious that
"Lenin's Observations On Bukharin's Book" was never again reissued in the press. Although the *Lenin's Collection* materials were
reprinted in toto in Volume V of Lenin's *Collected Works*, "Lenin's
Observations" are omitted. In explanation of this fact to an Old
Bolshevik, A. V. Snegov, the one-time deputy director of the Marx-
Engels-Lenin Institute, G. Obichkin stated that "Lenin didn't
always arrange his marginal notes too well."

In 1932 the State Technical-Theoretical Publishing House
printed another of Bukharin's books entitled *Studies*. The author included in this collection most of the articles and papers mentioned
above and also the text of a major speech given at the grand annual
meeting of the Academy of Sciences on the subject, "The Technology and Economics of Contemporary Capitalism," a paper called
"Darwinism and Marxism" read by Bukharin at a meeting held on
the fiftieth anniversary of Darwin's death, and also shorter articles,
"Valery Briusov and Vladimir Mayakovsky" and "Nasty Notes," a
piece on Yesenin which *Pravda* had published in 1932. This latter

article was included not only for reasons of thematic similarity;
Bukharin was not quite fair to Yesenin who has nowadays, so to
speak, come to life again. In 1932, however, the words with which
Bukharin ended his "Nasty Notes" were more topical:

It cannot be denied that Yeseninism is proving very popular and thus
becoming a harmful force in our society. It is beyond doubt that large
numbers of our Communist Youth are catching it too. What is it all
about? . . .

It is about the fact that we ourselves do not adequately understand the
ideological tasks in front of us. We are serving up the same old ideological
food. That doesn't mean simply that this food is cooked according to the old
Communist recipe . . . that recipe is a good one. But the fact is that the interests of the consumer are being forgotten: the consumer all too often gets
rubber-stamped paragraphs and circulars written in such an unbelievably
boring and monotonous style that it would make someone not used to them
throw up. . . .

Life in this transitional age is so luxuriant and so complex, it is so
chockablock with contradictions and conflict, social ones, day-to-day ones,
personal ones, that there is plenty of scope for drama, tragedy, comedy,
lyricism, for the fullest development of the interests of science and philosophy—for everything that has been labeled man's "spiritual cultivation." But
even here, in our country, there is a discrepancy between mass require-
ments and quality of production.

What is the appeal of Yesenin for our youth? . . . Why is it that our
Komsomol member so often uses his copy of *A Communist's Companion* to
cover up a little book of Yesenin's poems? Because we, and our men of
ideas, have not touched the strings of our youth that have been touched—
albeit in an essentially pernicious way—by Sergei Yesenin. . . . At this
point let me address a few words to our proletarian poets. "How often has
the world been told . . ." that the present shift of poets is dealing with the
wrong things. Every poet has turned into a critic, an organizer, and a politician at the cost of studying real life, at the cost of scrutinizing himself, at the
cost of making contact with the masses whom he should represent with his
living poet's voice. And when life asserts itself and they try to "sing" it turns
out that their lyricism (even with the most intransigent among them) is sing-
ing with an alien voice.

It is worth adding that Sergei Yesenin had the greatest respect
for Bukharin. In one of his poems written in 1924 about the home-
less orphans who were wandering about the country in hundreds of
thousands Yesenin wrote:

Comrades, today I come to you in grief.
It has returned, that pain which I have missed.
I know a story sad beyond belief—
The unforgettable *Oliver Twist*.

Oh I grew up like them, skinny and sad,
The dawn was very thin and very cold.
But if they all lined up there, every lad,
They'd sing as poets do, a thousandfold.

They're Pushkin, Lermontov, Nekrasov, and Koltsov.
Bukharin, Trotsky, Lenin, and I are in their places.
And how shall these poor verses sound sorrowful enough
In contemplation of their mucky faces?

I sing to those who creep in boilers for a bed.
For those who sleep in sorting bins I sing.
If only they could hear! In verse let it be said
That some of us are wounded by their suffering.

(Translated from the version included in S. Yesenin, *Sobraniye sochineniy*, Gosizdat 1926, vol. 2, 108–9. In all modern editions the words about Bukharin, Trotsky, and Lenin are omitted.)

Bukharin not only read and studied poetry, he was friends with many poets. And not only proletarian poets like Demyan Bedny. Bukharin was a great admirer and willing supporter of as strikingly unproletarian a poet as Osip Mandelstam whose widow writes in her memoirs:

In 1922 O.M. was anxious to help his brother Yevgeniy who had been arrested. That was when he first turned to Bukharin. We visited him in the Metropole Hotel. Nikolai Ivanovich rang Dzerzhinsky immediately and asked him to see O.M. A meeting was fixed for the following morning. Dzerzhinsky received O.M. informally and suggested he might stand surety for his brother. In fact this suggestion was put to him by Bukharin. Dzerzhinsky gave the investigator immediate instructions. Next morning O.M. went to see the investigator and returned full of impressions. The investigator had been armed, in uniform and flanked by two bodyguards. "The instructions have come through" he had said, "but we're not letting your brother out on bail." Reason for refusal: "It will be embarrassing for us to have to arrest you if your brother commits another crime. . . ." The implication was that some crime had already been committed. "Another crime?" said O.M. when he got home, "What have they got him on?" We didn't trust them an inch and our fear was that they were about to "hang something" on Yevgeniy. It then occurred to us that when Dzerzhinsky had given his instructions by telephone he had used a tone which didn't oblige the investigator to do anything at all.

Once Bukharin learned from O.M. of his reception by the investigator he flew into a rage. We were taken aback by the way he reacted. And two days later he came to tell us that no crime had been committed, not an original one and not another one; Yevgeniy would be released in a day or two. These extra days were necessary to complete and close the file dealing with the noncommission of a crime. . . .

For all the bright spells in his life O.M. was indebted to Bukharin. His 1928 book of poetry would never have seen the light of day but for the active involvement of Nikolai Ivanovich who managed to get Kirov on their side. The trip to Armenia, the flat, our ration cards, contracts for future publications (which never came about but which were paid for—and that was vital because they were starving O.M. to death by preventing him from getting work)—all of this was managed by Bukharin.

In the thirties Bukharin began complaining that he was short of "transmission belts." His influence was on the wane and he was in fact almost completely isolated. But he never hesitated to try and help O.M. and racked his brains over whom to approach and through whom one should get things done.[4]

Bukharin was also very friendly with Maxim Gorky, a writer different from Mandelstam in his opinions and personal qualities and whom Mandelstam did not get on with. Bukharin was a regular visitor at Gorky's house; the latter was very fond of gathering a lot of writers around himself. Sometimes Bukharin ran across Stalin at Gorky's: Stalin was another regular visitor who used to drop in without warning. On the first floor of Gorky's fine house a sumptuous dinner would be served on evenings such as those. Writers and other visitors were invited to dine. Anyone not invited would have to stay in the downstairs rooms—Stalin's guards would not let them leave before Stalin himself went home.

The dramatic events taking place in the countryside in the early thirties brought people in their hundreds and thousands legging it into Moscow from the outlying countryside and provincial towns. Many of them went to Kalinin, the head man of the union. But many others, too, wanted to see Gorky, the protector of the poor, downtrodden, and famished. This led to a guard being placed around Gorky's house and permission to enter was very restricted.

One Ukrainian writer spent three nights outside Gorky's house before she managed to see him and tell him all about the famine in the Ukraine. One day Bukharin decided to call and see Gorky, but he was stopped by the guards. He wasn't carrying his identification as a member of the Central Committee and he had not bothered to ring Gorky in advance and arrange a pass. Walking around to the back of the house, without more ado, he climbed over the high wall, but even then he was stopped by two guards. Gorky's secretary came out to see what all the fuss was about, recognized Bukharin, and told them to let him in at once. It is doubtful whether Gorky and Bukharin ever found it particularly pleasant to recall this incident.

At the end of March 1928 on the occasion of Gorky's sixtieth birthday when he was about to return once and for all to the Soviet Union Bukharin wrote an article in *Pravda* entitled "What Do We Want from Gorky?" It included the following passage:

> Building goes ahead rapidly. Our Soviet anthill is bustling as never before. People are turning over great big stones, they are doing silly things and making mistakes, then correcting them, making more mistakes and correcting them again, learning, renewing everything around them, renewing themselves—and yet we still haven't got the wide fabric of this great age. Attempts are being made, but they're a bit weak. More often than not we hear either grumbling or one hundred percent ecstatic cries from one hundred percent cast-iron, hard-metal, steel-clad proletarian writers who have no organic network of varying types but only artificial dummies to be fitted out according to normal instructions. . . . If only we had some good criticism. It has yet to be born. What we do have are loudmouths who'll expose some form of deviation before you can say Jack Robinson. . . . Much that is good is being born now. But we can say of this literary "country of ours" that, though it is not small and is not abundant, "yet there is no order in it."
>
> Gorky, with all his great gifts, can fill an enormous gap. He is awaited, as their very own creative artist, by this Soviet Union of ours, our working class, our Party with whom Gorky was connected over many, many years. This is why we eagerly await his arrival. He is coming to us to do a job, to do a great and good, glorious job of work.[5]

In the event, given the circumstances of the 1930s, Gorky proved incapable of adequately justifying the high expectations of his friends.

At this point in the narrative, something should be said of

the relations between Bukharin and A. Lunacharsky. The latter, it will be remembered, was a bosom friend of Lenin's and was commissar for education not only in the first Soviet government but under every subsequent Council of People's Commissars. In the 1920s the Commissariat for Education assumed control for all schools and technical institutions, the whole of higher education, all the theatres, libraries, and museums. Lunacharsky, in other words, was more than just a high-ranking state leader, he was one of the most outstanding creators of the new Soviet culture. He was the organizer and theoretician behind the new nationwide system of education, he was an expert on literature and art, a writer and dramatist, a Marxist philosopher and a historian. Like Bukharin he was one of the first Bolshevik Communists to achieve full membership of the Academy of Sciences, though Lunacharsky belonged to the older generation of the Party intelligentsia, having begun to work for the Social Democratic movement in Russia ten years before Bukharin—a matter of real significance at that time. Another difference was that Lunacharsky came from the family of a prominent civil servant in the Czarist administration whereas Bukharin was the son of a small-time clerk and teacher. Bukharin had a good grammar school record and got through half the course at Moscow University but his childhood had been spent playing with "street children." Lunacharsky, on the other hand, was given a magnificent education in Europe—studying in France and Italy, and then reading natural sciences and philosophy at Zurich University. In many respects he was a man of better education and greater talents than Bukharin. Among friends and relations he was prone to speak dismissively about Bukharin as a cultural figure and he had no high opinion of his works on economics. He was annoyed by Bukharin's straightforwardness and displeased by his frequent use of unprintable language which, incidentally, was the general practice in Party circles during those years.

On the other hand Bukharin stood incomparably higher than Lunacharsky in the Party hierarchy. Lunacharsky never served on the Central Committee, whereas Bukharin became a member of this body as early as 1917 and was also in the Politburo for ten years. Bukharin was the man who, in the late 1920s, issued directives on

questions of culture and education which were binding on Lunacharsky himself, though Bukharin never played upon his Party sen-
iority, always admitting the other's superiority in many cultural
areas and consulting him frequently. Conflict would sometimes
arise between the two men in Bukharin's capacity as editor of *Pravda,* and this would generally be settled not in the Politburo but in
the flat belonging to Klara Tsetkin who was thirty years older than
the one and forty years older than the other. Throughout the 1920s
Klara Tsetkin lived most of the time in Moscow rather than Germany in charge of the female secretariat of the Comintern. Bukharin
used to go with his friend Karl Radek to visit Lunacharsky at his
home and return visits were paid to Bukharin's flat in the House of
Soviets, now the Metropole Hotel.

Lunacharsky was "disgraced" in 1929, the year which saw Bukharin sacked from the Politburo as leader of "rightist" deviation.
Lunacharsky had disagreed with a number of decisions taken by the
Central Committee on questions of education, especially the short-
ening and simplifying of courses in the trade-training technical colleges. Dismissed from his position as commissar for education, Lunacharsky then spent some years as head of the academic council of
the USSR Central Executive Committee and in 1933 he was appointed Soviet ambassador to Spain. However, on the way to Ma-
drid Lunacharsky died suddenly at the age of fifty-eight in the small
French town of Menton. When news of his death reached Moscow
Bukharin wrote a long obituary, "A Shining Talent," which was published in *Izvestiya.* Here is an extract from the article:

Anatoliy Vasilyevich Lunacharsky was one of the most gifted personalities brought to prominence by the working-class movement in our country.
His was a truly shining talent. He was a bright star shooting across the blue
sky, a man of quite unusual and many-sided gifts, rich in cultural experience, brilliant in artistic ability. He lacked the iron character, the strength,
the will, the stamina essential to a true leader of millions of men. He lacked
also the theoretical profundity, the orthodox spirit, and the indomitable
power of argument which distinguished the true geniuses of the proletarian
revolution. By nature a gentle, artistic person, Lunacharsky fell frequently
into tremendous vacillation and meandering and although he never laid
claim to roles that were beyond him, his political biography is riddled with
serious failures. Nevertheless this warrior in the service of our Party spent

his whole life as one of the noblest knights of the proletarian revolution and his name without any doubt will go down in history as that of a fiery warrior and eager builder in the cause of socialist culture.[6]

Lunacharsky's body was brought home quickly from France to Moscow. He was given a state funeral and his ashes, borne by members of the Soviet government, were immured in the Kremlin wall. After the funeral, however, there were only two people who visited the family of Lenin's dead comrade-in-arms, Kamenev and Bukharin.

Bukharin had been busily occupied in the early 1930s by a considerable amount of vital business but now he found he had more time for relaxation, more time to devote to what are now called hobbies. Ever since childhood Bukharin had loved sketching and painting. He had discovered in himself a real talent for art without having the opportunity to develop it because his father's family was always in dire need. Later on Bukharin would come to devote some of his time and energies to a study of the theory and history of art. He was particularly fond of sketching people whom he knew and he would indulge himself in this way at many a conference, congress, or plenary session. Sometimes he drew landscapes, sketches of places which he happened to be visiting. His works were far from being masterpieces, as he well knew. Painting was a form of relaxation for him just as violin-making was for Mikhail Tukhachevsky.

When dealing with Bukharin's life and activities in 1931–33 one can scarcely ignore an episode as significant for him as the publication in late summer 1933 of a short pamphlet entitled *V. I. Lenin: Observations On Bukharin's Article On the State* (Party Publishing House, Moscow). This edition was a kind of answer to the publication two years earlier of Lenin's observations on Bukharin's book about the economics of transition, and the two pamphlets were so closely similar in appearance that one could have been mistaken for the other. The new one was devoted to the correspondence between Lenin, Zinoviev, and Bukharin in 1916 arising from the latter's article, "Toward a Theory of the Imperialist State," one of his very first excursions into theory. It was Lenin's view that the article contained a number of inaccuracies, that it was too "legal" in its treatment, and that some of the ideas advanced in it needed "close scrutiny." For these reasons he opposed its publication in the illegal journal *Social-Democrat Miscellany*. Nevertheless Lenin was extremely cautious in his criticism and when writing to Zinoviev he made specific recommendations as to the tone and character of the rejection notice to be sent to Bukharin by the editors. Lenin drafted this letter himself.

Dear Comrade,
     We regret to inform you that your article, "Toward a Theory of the Imperialist State" cannot be given space. As it happens, Russian material takes up so much space that other themes are severely restricted and there is simply not enough money. However that is not the main point: your article does contain the following shortcomings.
     The title does not relate to the contents. The article consists of two parts which are not properly joined together: Part One, about the state in general, and Part Two about state capitalism and its growth (especially in Germany). The second part is good and useful but nine tenths of it is legally acceptable. We would advise you to make one or two minimal revisions and then have it published in one of the legal journals. We should be pleased to give you every assistance toward publication in this way. The first part touches upon a subject of the gravest significance in principle but it does only touch upon it. In an annual publication it is not possible for us to print a piece on such a vital question of theory which has not been fully thought out. . . . Our advice is: rework into legal acceptability (a) the section on state capitalism and (b) the argument against Gumplovich & Co. *Give close scrutiny* to all the rest. This is our opinion.[7] [Italics are Lenin's.]

     This is not the place to go into the rights and wrongs of the disagreement between Lenin and Bukharin on the question of the state. In 1933 it was quite clear that not only Bukharin's ideas but Lenin's as well (according to his 1917 book, *The State and Revolution*) corresponded very little to the character and function of the Soviet state at its current stage of development. What was particularly striking, however, was the enormous disparity between Lenin's guarded criticism of the young Bukharin and the preface which the editors of the Party Publishing House in the Marx-Engels-Lenin Institute saw fit to append to the new edition. Here is an extract from it.

All the documents which we have gathered together here in booklet form contribute invaluably to the general Marxist-Leninist theory of the state and the dictatorship of the proletariat . . . the reinforcement of this dictatorship has been assuming special significance in view of the furious opposition shown by kulak elements to the all-out socialist offensive. The kulaks and the other forces of counterrevolution are down but not out and they are striving to undermine the Soviet state and the foundations of the dictatorship of the proletariat using a wide diversity of disguises. Kulak-type opposition manifests itself in those anti-Party factions, blatant agents of our enemies in the class struggle, who speak out against Lenin's Party and leadership. One such counterrevolutionary group, clearly an agency of the kulaks, was that of Ryutin and others, in which a prominent part was played by activists of the infamous "school" of Slepkov, Maretsky, etc. which culminated in collaboration with Kamenev and Zinoviev to arrange the outright betrayal of the working class.[8]

By "school" the writer meant to indicate the group of young "Red" professors which gathered around Bukharin in the late 1920s and, under his leadership, waged war actively against "leftist" opposition. Most of these young academics supported Bukharin in 1928–29. They then occupied prominent positions in the Soviet press, in the various organs of agitation and propaganda, and also in the foremost institutions of learning, including the Communist Academy and the Institute of Red Professors. Only one or two of the members of this group, such as A. Stetsky and V. Astrov, spoke out against Bukharin, and these two promptly began speeding up the Party hierarchy. Most of the other members of the "Bukharin school" lost their jobs and were even expelled from the Party. Thus it was that the publication of Lenin's letters in 1933 with such a tendentious preface represented a clear warning to Bukharin and a further attempt to pressure him.

Four

The Seventeenth Party Congress

———— >>> <<< ————

A FULL YEAR before the Seventeenth Party Congress
was due to take place provisional results of the First Five-Year Plan
were produced, in January 1933, for the joint plenary session of the
Central Committee of the Communist party and the Central Control Commission. This session met at a time of crisis in national agriculture comparable only to that of 1920–21. As we have seen, most
of the southern regions of the country were stricken with famine, although there was no mention of this in the press and no one spoke of
it from the platform of that meeting. Stalin read a speech in which
he made much of the country's successes in industry, blatantly exag-
gerating many of them. He also stressed the success of the collectivization of agriculture—by the beginning of 1933 no less than two
hundred thousand collective farms and something in the region of
five thousand state farms had been set up. He pointed out that during the period of the Five-Year Plan the countryside had taken de-
livery of a number of tractors and other pieces of agricultural machinery. The clear conclusion to be drawn from Stalin's address
might have been that the material situation of peasants and workers
during the Five-Year Plan had improved significantly, which was
clearly untrue. The statistics relating to agricultural production in
the 1930s, it was later discovered, had been drastically falsified—
the figures exaggerated agricultural production totals by a margin of

at least twenty percent.

However, statistics could not replace actual grain for food supplies or raw materials for light industry. Stalin did admit that grain
requisitioning had been more difficult in 1932 than in 1931, but he
failed to reveal the real reasons behind the shortages and actually
claimed that more grain had been produced in that year than in the
previous one. There was a greater degree of self-criticism in the
speech made by Stalin during debate on "Work in the countryside,"
though even here he glossed over many crucial aspects of the current situation.

Dissatisfaction at the country's desperate economic plight gave
rise to the formation of further oppositional factions, even in the
Party leadership. For instance, the January plenary session of the
Central Committee condemned the faction of N. Eysmont, G. Tolmachov, and A. P. Smirnov which had not only opposed Politburo
policy on a wide range of issues but had actually demanded the
removal of Stalin from the leadership. The most substantial member
of this group was Aleksandr Petrovich Smirnov, an Old Bolshevik
from a poor peasant background who had taken part actively in the
first Revolution of 1905 and had been a delegate to the Fourth and
Fifth Congresses of the Russian Social Democratic Workers' party.
He was elected to the Party Central Committee as early as the
Prague Conference along with Stalin and well before most of the
other members attending that plenary session. During the civil war
he worked for the People's Commissariat for Internal Affairs
(NKVD) and the Commissariat for Production, later becoming gen-
eral secretary of the Peasants' International and secretary to the
Central Committee itself. As distinct from his namesake, Ivan
Nikitich Smirnov, he had never before joined an oppositional group
and was widely respected among the Bolshevik party activists.

The discussions conducted at the January plenary session were
not published either then or later. There is evidence that no less a
person than Kirov made a number of damaging criticisms at the conference. An exception was made in the case of Bukharin, Rykov, and
Tomsky who were invited to speak and whose addresses were published in January 1933. In his address Bukharin condemned the ac-

tivities of the Smirnov group and also mentioned his own responsibility for "rightist" opposition in the Party during 1928–29, for which he had formulated the theoretical basis. After mentioning the Party's great successes in the implementation of the Five-Year Plan he went on to claim that they were still "at war" and therefore demanded unity and solidarity at the expense of all opposition. "It's a simple question," he said, "you are either for the Party or against the Party and there can be no in-between positions." Time had settled all previous differences and difficulties since "we have become a new country by virtue of our technological capability, a new country by virtue of our economic structure and system, a new country by virtue of our fresh alignment of the forces of class."[1] However, the self-criticism indulged in by Bukharin and more especially by Rykov and Tomsky, was deemed insufficient, as the resolution taken by the plenary session made clear. As to Smirnov, he was expelled from the Central Committee but not from the Party. Eysmont and Tolmachov were expelled from the Party.

In January 1934 the Seventeenth Party Congress was held and it came to be known in Party history as the "Congress of Victors." It was indeed true that after the arduous, complex struggle which went on in the country between 1930 and 1933 the Party ultimately won out. The "revolution from above" proclaimed by Stalin in 1929 had taken place. Opposition from the kulaks and from Nepman profiteers had been routed along with that shown by large sections of the middle peasantry. The overwhelming majority of the peasants had joined collective farms. The rate of participation in the socialist system was over eighty percent in the countryside and had reached ninety-nine percent in the cities. Hundreds of new plants and factories had come into operation and all over the country new branches of industry had opened: machine tool construction, car and aviation industries, the production of turbines and generators, high-quality steel, combine-harvesters, synthetic rubber, and the like.

On the other hand, in many regions the success of the Party had been obtained at too high a price. The consequences of the class struggle in the countryside recalled the atrocities of the civil war. Agricultural output in 1933 was still falling: it was five percent down in 1932 and twenty percent down in 1928; the total grain harvest in the period 1929–33 was lower than in 1909–13. In 1933 the nation saw half the head of cattle it achieved in 1913, pigs had fared almost as badly over the same period and horses even worse. It was true that the basic sections of heavy industry had increased four or five times by the end of the Five-Year Plan as compared with 1913 but in light industry growth had been achieved only in goods such as watches, knitted goods, tinned goods, etc. Sugar production was sixty percent of the output in 1913; meat, fifty-seven percent; woolen goods, eighty-six percent. In 1932 cotton fabrics alone had reached the level of 1928, itself four percent down from 1913. The standard of living of the population remained extremely low and fell far short of the minimal levels set by the First Five-Year Plan.

Party functionaries, especially in the provinces, were worn out: in many sectors of the population there was a grumbling discontent and this was reflected even in the Party. Among Party activists just before the Seventeenth Congress a secret opposition to Stalin's leadership was growing. Bukharin, however, was not in the conspiracy of opposition. We have already seen that he was not elected as delegate to the Sixteenth Congress and did not attend despite his membership of the Central Committee. In the election of delegates to the Seventeenth Congress Bukharin once agin failed to be chosen by any of the Party organizations but he decided nevertheless that he would attend the congress and even accept an invitation to speak in support of the Party line and Stalin in particular. He agreed, moreover, to refer to his "rightist" errors, something he had refused to do in 1930–31. Speaking at the fifth meeting of the congress, he had this to say:

Despite the fact that for some years now I have been actively following the general Party line, at this congress, a congress of totaled accounts, I consider it necessary to draw attention to certain relevant conclusions. In the first place, it is clear that the "rightist" movement to which I once belonged pursued a different political line, a line at variance with the all-out Communist offensive, at variance with the new onslaught against capitalist elements which was being waged by the Party. It is further clear that this line envisaged different rates of development, that in effect it opposed the enforced development of industrialization, opposed the extraordinary and acutely bitter struggle which found expression in the slogan "liquidate the kulak class!"; it opposed the policy of transforming small-scale peasant farming; it shrank from tackling the problems created by the inevitable aggravation of the class struggle in which this very aggravation was not just a chance event but was rooted in logical development, the logical development of contradictions initiated by NEP; it opposed every new stage of the broad socialist offensive, failing to comprehend its historical inevitability and drawing conclusions which could only be construed as anti-Leninist. . . . It emerges clearly that this group inevitably became the center of attraction for all those forces which fought against the socialist offensive, namely the kulak strata in the first place and on the one hand, and, on the other, their theoretical adherents among the intelligentsia. Equally clearly it emerges in the light of subsequent events that victory of that deviationist group would necessarily have unleashed a third force, would have weakened in the extreme the positions of the working class and the proletariat leading to premature intervention from outside, which was already creeping up on . . .the weaker, less healthy parts, and thereby to the restoration of capitalism as the net result of the exacerbation of our situation at home and abroad, by ensuring the significant erosion of the strength of the proletariat and unleasing the forces of antiproletarian counterrevolution. . . . It further emerges that Comrade Stalin was entirely correct in speaking out so eloquently, making brilliant use of Marxist-Leninist dialectics, against many of the theoretical premises of rightist deviation which I myself had previously formulated. Under this heading I shall cite the following: the so-called theory of equilibrium, the theory of organized capitalism, the theory of the incorporation of kulak elements into socialism, the theory of the fading class struggle, and the theory of commodity circulation and the market as the decisive and fundamental means of transforming the peasant economy. It is clear that he was right in simultaneously shattering the corresponding attempts to create factions—which flowed naturally from those theoretical positions and proceeded according to a particular political orientation—by eradicating right-wing opposition.[2]

Bukharin could scarcely have been sincere in saying all this but sometimes it is necessary to act against one's conscience. This speech was the price which Bukharin was prepared to pay now in the interests, as he thought, of Party unity. He was not looking for personal advantage, was not stipulating certain conditions by which to regain a post of responsibility. It seems probable that, realizing the full complexity of the situation of the USSR at home and abroad (though not realizing the aims and secret designs in Stalin's mind)

Bukharin wanted in one way or another to help the Party.

The battle for collectivization certainly had ended in victory for the Party. At the time Bukharin had openly opposed the battle itself, seeking a smoother, more evolutionary transition to a socialistic rural economy. He was opposed to violence on a massive scale, to the compulsion visited upon the kulaks, to the method of kulak-liquidation employed by Stalin. The battle nevertheless went ahead and both victors and vanquished were to emerge from it with many bleeding wounds. What was the point of arguing about how Party policy might have been best constructed five or six years earlier? The thing to do now was to set about healing the wounds and finding a way toward a new economic upturn in industry and agriculture.

Bukharin's speech made it plain that he was much concerned over the international position of the USSR. Fascism had won the day in Germany; in Japan extreme, militaristic, right-wing forces had come to power. Bukharin had read *Mein Kampf* and it was his belief that Hitler's words on the subject of living space to be found in the east were more than mere propaganda. He quoted Hitler from the congress platform:

We are now completing the perpetual movement of the Germans southwards and westwards in Europe and are turning our eyes to the lands in the east. We are coming to the end of a policy of colonial trade and moving over to a policy of fighting for new lands. And when we speak of new land in Europe we can be thinking only of Russia and her dominions. . . . Our future foreign policy must have as its aim not merely a western or eastern orientation; it must be an eastern policy in the sense of appropriating the territory which is so essential to the German people.

From the same platform he read out the lofty phrases of a number of Japanese generals concerning their plans for the "emancipation" of Siberia. "So this is how things stand," Bukharin concluded. "Hitler is formulating his brazen, criminal policy in such a way as to squeeze us out into Siberia. The Japanese militarists are formulating theirs in such a way as to try to squeeze us out of Siberia. So it seems that we shall have to find somewhere in one of the blast-furnaces in Magnitka to house all 160 million inhabitants of our Union."[3]

Faced with this mortal danger, Bukharin was suggesting, all differences within the Party must be temporarily suspended and the need was for unity around the existing leader, and that meant Stalin. And so he had come to the conclusion that the best form of conduct for himself and his recent friends must be a policy of the utmost loyalty to Stalin and the current Party leadership. None of the former opposition members and none of Stalin's present comrades-in-arms, no one suspected that Stalin would use this ominous outside peril as a pretext and cover for the extermination of his former opponents and almost the entire rearguard of the Party.

Five

Nikolai Bukharin as Editor of *Izvestiya*

--------≫≫≪≪--------

THE ERSTWHILE LEADERS OF "rightist" opposition were reelected to the Party Central Committee at the Seventeenth Congress but as candidates rather than full members. Another person elected to candidate status was G. Sokolnikov, one of the former leaders of "leftist" opposition. As before, Rykov was given the office of commissar for communications (or, as it was then called, people's commissar for post and telephones). Tomsky was a success in his office as head of state publishing; for some reason many people imagined that he would not be able to cope with the work, but in this respect he let them down. Bukharin's position was different. His slight demotion in the Party hierarchy coincided with a return to actual political activity. On 22 February 1934 on the back page of the newspaper *Izvestiya* the words "Editor : I. M. Gronsky" were replaced by "Editor : N. I. Bukharin," and that issue included a resolution of the presidium of the USSR Central Executive Committee "to appoint N. I. Bukharin as editor-in-chief for the newspaper *Izvestiya*, organ of the Central Executive Committee of the USSR and the All-Union Central Executive Committee." Gronsky was to be relieved of his duties as editor of *Izvestiya* but allowed to continue as editor-in-chief of the journal *Novy Mir*.

The newspaper *Pravda*, which Bukharin had once been in charge of, was, of course, an organ of the Party Central Committee itself and its articles amounted to directives issued by the Party. Work on the less official newspaper *Izvestiya*, however, opened up new possibilities for a journalist and publicist, possibilities which would have been hard to discover working for *Pravda*. Bukharin aimed to turn *Izvestiya* into an interesting newspaper and in this he succeeded. In that year, 1934, it became the most popular and widely read of all Soviet newspapers, although later on, and especially in 1936, the standard was to fall quite severely. A second aim of the new editor was to give his newspaper a more decisive anti-Fascist stance, and this was also achieved. At the same time he attempted to contrast socialist humanitarianism with Fascist barbarism.

Bukharin soon became very popular among the staff of the newspaper. He proved straightforward and easily accessible and did not stand on ceremony. More than that, he clearly knew about newspapers and loved them, and possessed vast erudition matched with a great capacity for hard work. He took an interest in every section of the paper and was a frequent visitor to the printroom where copy was set up in type and run off to produce the fresh pages of *Izvestiya*. One former employee on the paper, M. D. Baitalsky, recalled those days in his memoirs:

Everyone realized that the new appointment had gone to that man of the unwinking eye—Bukharin, the one-time favorite of the Party. That was what Lenin had called him, with good reason,—and he soon proved popular in the editorial office. He was a man with a brilliant mind, many-sided education, a totally democratic spirit and not a trace of pretentiousness. No tension about him, no officiousness—a natural, straightforward manner and a knack of approaching people without condescending to them but, on the contrary, raising them to his own level in the only way possible, by respecting their dignity as human beings. The school created by the old Russian revolutionary intelligentsia cannot but make its mark.

He was the very image of a Party *intelligent* of earlier days, with his thin, little wedge-shaped beard, his ever-baggy jacket and lithe movements. He seemed always to walk very quickly because of his short stature. Anyone could enter his room at any time unannounced. Except that he wasn't always in his room—he could often be found leaning over someone else's desk glancing at galley-proofs and making swift but telling comments. As an editor he had no equal: he could catch his authors' ideas in a split sec-

ond and would amaze them with the speed and precision with which he
sorted the wheat from the chaff, abbreviating articles without spoiling anything in them. He was a good reader; he was a good writer, too.

Much of his writing was done on the edge of someone else's desk in the
noisiest room in the office. Under his regime at *Izvestiya* there was none of
the sacred observance of sluggish procedure which in the guise of "imitating
the boss" insinuates itself into every large-scale institution, not excluding
editorial offices. . . .

The typesetters expressed their satisfaction with him by making him a
special case: they accepted articles from him without having them typed up.
He wrote quickly and neatly, without crossing-out. As a theoretician
Bukharin made many mistakes but those who knew him could not imagine
Nikolai Ivanovich working with a staff of advisers prompting him to fine
phrases and literary models. He did his own thinking, he did his own writing, and when he did make mistakes they were mistakes arising from his
own mind, a powerful, inquisitive mind, inclined to soar away to distant
(perhaps too distant) regions. He never foisted his own mistakes on to other
people; he was simply not that kind of man. . . . Vain people like to make a
show of infallibility—Nikolai Ivanovich didn't have a trace of vanity. . . . It
goes without saying that he never read his speeches from notes.[1]

Bukharin retained all the main staff of the newspaper and at the
same time persuaded many celebrated writers and able journalists
to write more actively. His paper began regularly to print articles by
Maxim Gorky, Lev Kassil, Korney Chukovsky, and Demyan Bedny;
other frequent contributors included Laninsky, Ehrenburg, Gne-
din, the brothers Tur, and Leykin. However, the leading writer was
without doubt Karl Radek whose long articles appeared weekly,
sometimes twice a week. An experienced politician, something of a
cynic even, a talented publicist, a man of intelligence and real wit,
Karl Radek had started his writing career as a young socialist working for the Social Democratic press in Poland—and in both the Russian and German sections of that divided country. Right from the
first he stood out as a brilliant journalist and politician; his articles
began to appear in the German press as well. In Switzerland during
the First World War he met Lenin who acknowledged his various
talents but did not think much of him as a man or a politician, as can
be seen from some of his letters to Inessa Armand. Following the
February Revolution Radek left Switzerland for Russia along with

Lenin but stayed on in Sweden as an agent of the Central Committee because of his Austrian citizenship. After the October Revolution he moved on to Petrograd. He took part in the negotiations over the Treaty of Brest-Litovsk, protested about it and then, in 1918, joined Bukharin's faction of Left Communists which went out of existence following the revolution in Germany. He was sent by Lenin, along with Bukharin, Ioffe, and Rakovsky, to the first congress of German Soviets in Berlin. He was arrested in Germany and spent almost a year in gaol. As one of the organizers of the German Communist party he naturally attended its first congress. Later on he returned to Russia and became an active worker in the recently established Comintern. From 1924 he was one of the most vigorous members of the "leftist" opposition. It was Radek who was credited with the authorship of most of the extremely witty and malicious jokes about Stalin which spread like wildfire through the Party intelligentsia in the 1920s. As a member of the left, Radek naturally took issue with Bukharin in no uncertain terms. When the opposition had been routed Radek was sent into exile but in the late 1920s he was one of the first to surrender to Stalin and return to Moscow. He made a public denunciation of Trotsky and then proceeded to lavish praise on Stalin in his writings and even in private conversation.

Most of Radek's *Izvestiya* articles discussed problems of international significance and, first and foremost, the struggle against fascism and the threat of war. One or two articles by Kamenev and Preobrazhensky were published in 1934 and Bukharin's own pieces appeared frequently. In March of that year a long article of his entitled "The Crisis of Capitalist Culture and Problems of Culture in the USSR" was spread over three editions (6, 18, and 30 March) and 12 May saw the publication of another one, "Economics in a Soviet country." One more worthy of mention is his "How the World Will Be" published in the anniversary issue of 7 November 1934. Bukharin's pen was responsible for many a leading article and editor's piece. All these articles spoke eloquently of the author's vast erudition, though they lacked his earlier independence of mind and keen inquisitiveness.

It can be taken for granted that it was impossible at that time to hold down the job of editing a central newspaper without making a lot of compromises. For example, *Isvestiya* joined with the other media to facilitate the inflation of the cult of Stalin. Bukharin himself was the author of an article celebrating the tenth anniversary of the publication of Stalin's pamphlet, *On the Foundations of Leninism.* Another special article was devoted to the fifteenth anniversary of the defeat of Denikin which apparently came about by means of a "calculated plan of Stalin's amounting to a stroke of genius." But, of course, Bukharin had already described Stalin, at the Seventeenth Party Congress, as "the glorious field-marshall of the proletarian powers, the cream of the cream in revolutionary leadership." It was Bukharin's wish to remain unswervingly loyal to Stalin and the new Party leadership, though occasionally a critical remark would slip out, especially when he was among people he could trust. M. D. Baitalsky, an ex-Trotskyite of the twenties, recalls Bukharin describing Stalin as a plagiarist in the summer of 1934. It is not difficult to imagine what Bukharin thought of the confidential instructions issued to the main organs of the Soviet press with regard to the publication of photographs of Stalin. The retouchers were to increase the size of his forehead by one or two centimeters; a high forehead had long been considered a sign of intelligence and this was a cause of envy in the low-browed Stalin.

Bukharin looked after his colleagues on the newspaper and would often take trips into the countryside with them on their day off. There they would find all sorts of ways of amusing themselves and these sometimes included a holiday "bouncing" for the boss. They would throw him up in the air and catch him again—their own way of expressing gratitude for his friendliness.

His works on *Izvestiya* inevitably involved the renewal of many former contacts with various individuals and organizations. During this period Bukharin's interests were not directed toward economics; aside from the overriding international problems he was mainly interested, as before, in literature and poetry in particular. We have already seen that one of the poets particularly valued and protected by Bukharin was Osip Mandelstam. In 1933 Mandelstam wrote a poem about Stalin. It was not written down but simply dictated at various times to friends. Here is one of the variants of that poem.

> Without sense of our land we are living today
> And our words are inaudible ten yards away.
> But a half-conversation fulfills
> The man from the Georgian hills.
>
> Like worms are his fingers, as fat and as podgy,
> His words weigh like dumbbells, as true and as stodgy;
> His smile and his polished boots flash
> Like his long, creepy-crawly moustache.
>
> His leaders surround him like scraggy-necked boys;
> He treats his obsequious sub-men like toys.
> They whoop, weep, and whine—they're fine fellows,
> And he simply blusters and bellows.
>
> Like a blacksmith he forges his chains of decrees
> And he pokes and he knees and he gouges with these.
> He will torture and murder with zest
> And he sticks out his bumpkin's fat chest.

Someone denounced Mandelstam. In May 1934, soon after he had struck Aleksei Tolstoi across the face following a quarrel, he was arrested. Nadezhda Mandelstam, his wife, turned to Bukharin for support. She writes in her memoirs:

I went to see Nikolai Ivanovich Bukharin in the first days. On hearing my news his face fell and he bombarded me with questions. I had not imagined that he could get so worked up. He ran up and down the vast room and stopped in front of me from time to time to ask me a routine question. . . . "Have you been to see him?" I had to explain to him that there was now no question of visits. He was not aware. . . . "Has he written something inflammatory, then?" I said no—just a few renegade poems, nothing worse than the ones Nikolai Ivanovich had read. . . . I was lying, and I'm ashamed of it to this day. But if I had told the truth then there would have been no "breathing-space in Voronezh." Is it necessary to lie? Can one lie? Is the "lie to save a life" justified? It is very nice to live in circumstances which don't call for lying. Does such a place exist anywhere? . . . Without lies I couldn't have survived in our terrible days. I have lied all my life, to my students, at work, to nice people whom I knew but couldn't trust completely—that means most of them. But nobody believed me anyway—it was the usual untruthfulness of our age, something akin to conventional politeness. I'm not ashamed of this kind of lying and I misled Bukharin quite deliberately in a cold, calculating manner—it wouldn't do to scare away our one and only protector. . . . This was different. . . . How could I not have lied?

Bukharin replied that he could not have been arrested just for slapping Aleksei Tolstoi across the face. When I told him about Tolstoi's threats and that one sentence (pronounced by Gorky): "We'll show him a thing or two about hitting Russian writers"—this had the necessary effect, he all but groaned. This man who had seen the inside of czarist prisons and had been a supporter in principle of revolutionary terror probably saw that day with particular clarity into his own future.

In those days when I was agitating on my husband's behalf I often went to see Nikolai Ivanovich. His secretary, Korotkova, used to meet me with a frightened, tender smile and hurry through to announce me. The office door would be flung open and Bukharin would be rushing out from behind his desk to greet me. "Any news? . . . No, not on my side either. . . . Nobody knows a thing." These were the last times we met. On the way from Cherdyn to Voronezh I called in briefly at the office of *Izvestiya*. "Oh, those awful telegrams you kept sending from Cherdyn!" said Korotkova, disappearing into the office. When she emerged she was almost in tears: "Nikolai Ivanovich won't see you . . . there was a poem. . . ." And I never saw her again. Later on he told Ehrenburg that Yagoda had recited the poem to Stalin from memory and that he had gotten scared and backed away. Before that he had done everything in his power and we had him to thank for getting the case reviewed.[2]

It seems more likely that Bukharin did not "get scared" but was simply offended that Nadezhda Mandelstam had deceived him all along the line. That was why he refused to see her. It was nevertheless because of Bukharin that in 1934 Mandelstam managed to avoid a severe sentence and was given "no more" than a three-year period of exile in Voronezh.

Six

The First Congress of Soviet Writers

—————— »»»««« ——————

A RESOLUTION to abolish the separate proletarian writers' associations VOAPP and RAPP was taken by the Party Central Committee in April 1932. Similar adjustments were recommended for the other branches of art—more specifically, the so-called Proletkult (Culture of the Proletariat) and all its organizations were to be joined together. The resolution pointed out that the separate organizations of proletarian writers had obstructed the natural development of Soviet literature and it was now time to bring together all the writers who supported the platform of Soviet power and who wished to further the building of socialism into a single union of Soviet writers "containing a Communist faction." A working party under the chairmanship of Maxim Gorky was set up to organize the first congress.

In years to come, under the conditions of mass repression and the Stalin personality cult, the existence of a single Writers' Union would serve to strengthen control over writers' activities. Besides which, in the course of time many of the aims and methods of the discontinued RAPP organization became standard practice in the running of the Writers' Union. Nevertheless in the early thirties most writers welcomed with enthusiasm the decision to form a general union. The resolution seemed likely to put an end to discrimination against many talented Soviet writers whom the RAPP organi-

zation refused to deem either Soviet or proletarian and whose work
was systematically attacked in many literary journals. It seemed
likely to put an end to the separation of writers into various cat-
egories, the first one reserved for those officially described as "proletarian," the next for the "peasant" writers, and the third for so-
called fellow-travelers, a pejorative term which was applied to the
majority of the most popular Soviet writers even in official documents. A good number of the greatest writers, including Bulgakov,
Akhmatova, Zamyatin, and even Aleksei Tolstoi were placed in the
category of "volte-face" writers, or, worse still, "internal émigrés."
Many others were simply described as "enemies of the people" according to the principle: "Who is not for us is against us."

The establishment of a unified association of authors ostensibly
gave all of them equal rights and dispelled the inferiority complex
which was being foisted upon many writers and poets. Hence the
First Congress of Soviet Writers was regarded as an important step
in the direction of a modest liberalization in Party policy toward literature. In the same way people envisaged the subsequent introduction of equal and secret balloting for election to all organs of
the Soviet state and also amendments to the regulations of the Communist party including the abolition of the section providing for the
separation of all persons joining the Party into four unequal cat-
egories.

The Writers' Congress began on 17 August 1934 in the Column
Room of the House of Unions and continued for fifteen days during
which time the building was surrounded by a crowd of festive Muscovites shouting greetings to the writers as they arrived. From the
very beginning the congress seemed to be justifying the highest
hopes. Among those elected to the presidium were not only the acknowledged leaders of "proletarian" literature but also many erstwhile "fellow travelers." Boris Pasternak sat alongside Demyan
Bedny and Aleksandr Bezymensky. Next to Panfyorov and Tikhonov sat as old a figure in Russian writing as A. S. Novikov-Priboy.
Aleksei Tolstoi and Ilya Ehrenburg sat beside Mikhail Sholokhov.
The unifying nature of the occasion was emphasized by the fact that
two most important papers were read at the congress by former

leaders of the opposition. Karl Radek spoke on "Contemporary World Literature and the Tasks of Proletarian Art" and Bukharin's paper was entitled "On Poetry, Poetics, and the Problems of Poetic Creativity in the USSR."

It was no chance event that Bukharin was selected to address the first congress. He had long experience in the evolution of Party policy on artistic literature and in the twenties his pen had produced plenty of articles on literature and literary policy. The most important of these are in the collection, *N. Bukharin: Questions of Culture Under the Dictatorship of the Proletariat* (State Publishing House, Moscow-Leningrad 1925). His articles appeared in *Red Virgin Soil* and *Revolution and Culture*, among other journals. Some of the critical problems of aesthetics are examined in his monograph Λ *Theory of Historical Materialism* the first edition of which saw the light of day in 1921. In volume one of the *Literary Encyclopedia*, published in 1929, the following assessment of Bukharin's position in regard to aesthetics and literature is given:

In his capacity as one of the leaders of the program for the building of socialism undertaken by the Soviet Union he has frequently commented both on questions of cultural development under the dictatorship of the proletariat and on issues concerning the Party's policy on art. According to him, "It is essential to cast an eye over these regions. . . ." In dealing with questions of culture in the transition period Bukharin has displayed extreme care, invariably stressing that cultural problems cannot be settled by the mechanical application of violence. He singles out as especially important in this regard the free interplay of competing creative skills. At a conference on Party policy on artistic literature in 1924 he protested against "cavalry charges" intended to solve a cultural problem which "ought to be settled in a cooperative manner following from intelligent critical comment." Competitiveness in production is the most important thing. At a literary conference held under the auspices of the Central Committee in February 1925 Bukharin stood up for the idea that cultural hegemony must be won by the proletariat only under conditions of quite open competition guaranteed within the framework of the Party leadership. Now that they have seized political power members of the proletariat should not automatically extend their authority into the realm of culture. It was Bukharin's opinion that the real difficulty here lay in the need for the proletariat "to move into the regions of literature, culture, etc. and there by the sweat of their own brows to earn for themselves the right to leadership in society."

Arguing from these premises Bukharin fought on two fronts in the battle over artistic policy: Communist arrogance and surrender were in his eyes equally harmful tendencies. For this reason he took issue with those in authority who attempted to "pulverize" any writer just because his artistic outlook was unacceptable to the proletariat. On the contrary, Bukharin held that literary leaders should confine themselves to issues of ideology in general: as to questions of form, style, and so on these should be left to open competition between separate groups and tendencies. At the same time he warned of the dangers of "brushing aside" the problems involved in the creation of proletarian culture: "We must not brush aside the need to protect what little shoots we have. We have no right whatsoever to brush this aside; quite the reverse, we must realize the full meaning of that principle of dynamism which at the end of the day comprises the very core of our being."

The *Literary Encyclopedia* had a very high opinion of Bukharin's own literary abilities. The article continues in this vein:

Bukharin is an outstanding publicist. A shrewd, fierce, merciless polemicist, he can rouse himself to great heights of emotion when discoursing on the role of the working class in contemporary history, on the prospects for the world revolutionary movement, on the new man being created by our age. His works are distinguished by faith in the new culture brought into being by the working class, a culture "beside which capitalist civilization will seem like the *Waltz of the Dogs* compared with the great heroic symphonies of Beethoven." . . . Bukharin's pamphlets, such as *Yechmeniada*, *On World Revolution*, *Our Country and Culture*, *An Answer to Academician Pavlov*, etc., are models of the art of polemics, arguing through a number of serious sociological problems. His masterful use of a wide range of stylistic devices like irony, sarcasm, metaphor, hyperbole, similes and rhetorical questions, does not prevent him from enjoying wide popularity. He knows the art of saturating his language with expressions borrowed from living colloquial speech, salty words and phrases drawn from the depths of working-class conversation, or, on other occasions, using strings of images borrowed from the finest literature.[1]

It follows that Bukharin, because of his attitude to literature and aesthetics, was eminently suited to carry out Party policy as expressed in the abolition of RAPP and the establishment of a single Union of Writers. Thus it came as no surprise that he was entrusted with one of the most significant speeches given at the first congress. When Bukharin advanced to the platform to address the nine-

teenth session of the congress the audience gave him a warm ovation. The popularity of a given speaker can be judged by remarks in
the shorthand report. The announcement of a speech by the Soviet
dramatist V. Ya. Kirpotin, for example, went unapplauded. A joint
address on the same topic apparently attracted "applause." Radek
and Panfyorov were also "applauded." No applause accompanied
the RAPP theoretician G. Lelevich or the literary scholar Luppol as
they came up to speak. "Prolonged applause" greeted Korney
Chukovsky and Otto Schmidt, the hero of the recently concluded
Chelyuskin epic. A speech made by the Central Committee Secretary A. Zhdanov, was accorded "stormy applause." Bukharin's appearance on the platform was greeted with nothing less than "prolonged stormy applause," exceeded only by the "standing ovation"
accorded to Maxim Gorky's arrival and the election of the honorary
presidium headed by Stalin.

Bukharin's address lasted for several hours. The first part was
devoted to philosophical problems arising from the theory of literature and especially to the essential nature of poetic creativity as a
particular reflection of reality, a particular form of thinking and
expression. The second part dealt with poetics as the technology of
poetic skill. The speaker himself jokingly warned about the content
of these first two sections:

> I must ask the audience to forgive me. They are going to find a certain
> amount of this rather tedious but the tedium, like evil, will throw into
> greater relief the good material which will follow in a section which will be
> less tedious and where I might run into some solid opposition.[2]

This second section was devoted to a survey of the underlying
tendencies in the development of Russian poetry, or rather Soviet
poetry, and to the works created by its chief representatives. It was
now impossible to get by without making value judgments and giving brief reviews and quotations; this meant taking issue with people and giving offence. In literature, especially poetry, objectivity is
difficult to achieve and it was inevitable that Bukharin's taste and
judgment would meet with anything but general agreement. Perhaps no speech at this congress was followed by more energetic and

impassioned debate than the one made by Bukharin. I personally lack the literary expertise to give a proper analysis of this speech, but there can be no doubt that its numerous profound and accurate observations on the works of several established twentieth-century Russian poets were accompanied frequently by primitive, over-simplified value-judgments straight from the arsenal of vulgar sociology. Blok, for instance, was described as "a lad who belonged properly to the old culture with a philosophy arising from religious and erotic mysticism, from a purified form of orthodoxy with a touch of Catholicism, from Slavophilism directed by populism," Briusov as "that former theorist from the upper echelons of the radical industrial bourgeoisie . . . that army commander of bourgeois literature who came over to us and died a party-member transferring to the camp of the victorious *hoi polloi*" and Sergei Yesenin as "a fine singer of songs but a theorist of the kulak philosophy whose poetical insides were filled with the poison of despair in the face of new stages of the great upheaval." Strangely enough, these "sociological testmonials" were certainly not what evoked the strongest objections from those who took part in the subsequent discussion.

Calling for a raising of the standards of skillful achievement in poetry Bukharin rated the work of Mayakovsky very highly indeed, referring to this poet as "a Soviet classic who lives on in virtually every young poet and whose poetic mastery and poetic devices have entered our literature never to disappear from it." Certain other poets, including Pasternak, Selvinsky, Tikhonov, and Aseyev, Bukharin assessed as "poets of the highest caliber" and "remarkable individuals in poetic achievement," though he had many substantial reservations about the content of the poems written by the first two. After lavishing praise upon Demyan Bedny he was careful to point out nevertheless that "this poet is not now taking account of the enormous changes which are occurring, of the unbelievable expansion of culture and its growing complexity. . . . For this reason he is getting out of date—therein lies the greatest danger for him." Similarly cautious, though not unjustified, remarks were made by Bukharin with regard to proletarian poets in the Communist Youth movement such as Bezymensky, Svetlov, Zharov, Utkin, and one or two others. By way of explanation of his criticism of so many Soviet poets he said bluntly that it was now time to measure the achievements of our poets against world standards, the same standards used to evaluate Pushkin, Goethe, and Heine:

From this standpoint we must, first of all, cast an eye on the level of achievement attained by our poetry. When we do so we shall see that we have fallen well behind, that we are now taking only the first steps down the historical global road toward a new poetic culture. Is it not true that the poetic material which lies at hand in the treasure-houses of our poetry is pale and squalid when compared with the titanic content of life itself? . . . Is it not true that the wonders of history are a closed book for our poets? . . . Is it not true that our poets have failed properly to assimilate the remarkable heritage deriving from the ancient skills of all times and peoples? . . . . All of this is true! A vicious, boorish provincialism still rules over us. Our poetry has yet to rise to a clear understanding of the meaning of our age. It has yet to understand its present position.[3]

Bukharin concluded with these words:

Comrades, I call upon you not to be offended by some of the embittered words which I have been addressing to you. Together let us be permeated by the spirit of this great age, so important in the history of mankind, let us also arrive together at this conclusion: we must move toward a great literature, a vast literature, a literature mighty in its content; toward a literature of effectiveness, a literature which will stand out by its skillful achievement like a mountain range in the history of mankind and the history of art!

I close with a slogan: "Comrades, be venturesome!"[4]

The shorthand report of the congress contains this comment immediately following Bukharin's address: "Tumultuous applause throughout the auditorium, turning into a standing ovation. Cries of 'Hurrah!' Everyone stands." There was only one other speech, that of Maxim Gorky, which ended in such a tumultuous tribute by the audience.

The ovation received by Bukharin from the Congress of Writers indicated the degree of popularity which he still enjoyed in wide circles of the Soviet intelligentsia and youth. This episode did not escape the attention of observers from abroad. It was, as always, accompanied by a host of rumors and legends in which fact and fiction are difficult to sort out. In his book *The Ruin of a Generation*

Iosif Berger cites a story recalled for him by one of Bukharin's followers whom the author came across in 1937 in one of Stalin's camps at Solovki.

> At the Writers' Congress Bukharin made his speech about poetry. It met with tumultuous applause, having been interrupted several times with loud cries of approval. When Bukharin finished speaking it seemed as if the ovation by the delegates would never die down. Bukharin stood there on the platform, pale and confused, seemingly scared to death. And when he went back to his place in the presidium he said quietly to one or two friends, "Do you know what you've just done? Signed my death warrant." That is what had happened. Bukharin's ovation could not have escaped Stalin's attention.[5]

I doubt very much whether Bukharin was "scared to death" by the ovation which he had received. In any event his subsequent pronouncements at the congress do not suggest any kind of fear. No doubt Stalin was informed of the ovation, but it still seems unlikely that Bukharin spoke the words attributed to him. August 1934 was a period of "liberalization" and death sentences were still comparatively far away. Even Kamenev and Zinoviev were restored to Party membership at that time and in the summer of that year two of the stoutest of Trotsky's former supporters, Sosnovsky and Rakovsky had returned to the Party, having made long-winded statements of their "errors."

There were in addition quite a lot of writers and poets, especially those recently involved in Proletkult, who refrained from applauding Bukharin. His criticism had offended many of them, though it was in fact largely justified. The first one to oppose Bukharin was the young, pretty undistinguished Aleksei Surkov. He came to the defence of "our young poets, living young workers who would one day be the representatives of our poetry and for whom the work of Boris Pasternak was an unsuitable reference point in their development."[6] Accusing Bukharin of allowing personal taste to affect his judgment of poetry Surkov spoke with some regret of the resurrection of the term "humanitarianism." This is what he said:

> Our congress has bestowed citizenship upon one word which we used to treat with mistrust and even enmity. That word is "humanitarianism." . . .

We were obliged, and we had the historical right, to despise and loathe
people using that word. And now here we are accepting it as an everyday
word. . . . There are those of our comrades who present humanitarianism
in the image of a brown-haired girl in a white dress . . . with delight in her
eyes, gazing into the Future (with a capital letter). I want to accept that
image but I cannot do so. . . . Something makes me sketch out the image of
humanitarianism for myself in a different form, perhaps rather cruder, but
in its crude flesh all the lovelier. . . .[7]

And Surkov went on to exemplify the image of humanitarianism
in the chairman of a provincial Security Section who had put in thir-
teen years service in the punitive organs.

And when he was asked by some of our friends belonging to the "morally pure" intelligentsia, "Tell us, when you are sending people off for execution didn't a feeling of humanitarianism awaken within you, didn't you at
least once put yourself in their place?" he would give a blunt, succinct
reply: "I've been in their place all my life. When a peasant out in the field
tears up goosefoot he doesn't ask whether it likes it or not. He just wants to
make sure his children don't starve!" . . . Eduard Bagritsky gave us the
model image of this humanitarianism in his poem

> . . . The age up the road awaits its entry
> In tense concentration, like a sentry.
> Be not afraid! Go, stand by its side.
> You are alone; the age be your guide.
> Stretch out your hand; your friends fly!
> Glance all around you; enemies still.
> And if the age tells you to lie, you lie!
> And if the age tells you to kill, you kill![8]

Given this kind of interpretation of humanitarianism it is natural
that the young Surkov could not find a reference point in the work of
Boris Pasternak, work which, to use Surkov's own phrases, could do
nothing more than "demagnetize the young Red Army-man's heart,
the flower of our youth, with the water of intimate lyricism."

Semyon Kirsanov was another person offended in the extreme
by Bukharin. With obvious distortion of the latter's words and ideas,
Kirsanov declared:

What a funny thing: according to Bukharin all the poets who have used
their verses to participate in the political life of our country are out of date,
masses of them, but the others are not out of date, the so-called pure (and

not so pure) lyric poets. . . . What strikes you as obvious in all this? It needs
to be stated bluntly and clearly: Bukharin's attempt to withdraw poetry
from its battle stations in real life, from stations where the poet can have an
effect on life today, and relegate it to a position right at the rear.[9]

There was nothing at all wrong in subjecting Bukharin, erstwhile
leader of the "rightists" and theorist of the kulaks, to criticism of this
kind. In any case, the criticism directed at him contained much that
was justified. A poet from Leningrad, Dmitri Petrovsky, was right
to describe Velemir Khlebnikov, whom Bukharin had scarcely even
mentioned, as "a genius of a poet, the greatest of revolutionaries in
poetic form and . . . a bold realist." After quoting several magnificent lines by this poet Petrovsky went on to say, "There are innumerable quantities of lines, stanzas, and whole poems like this in
Khlebnikov's work. Khlebnikov's laboratory experiments often
blended, and still blend with his actual finished poems. . . . With
Khlebnikov's magnificent work behind them the way was tremen-
dously smoothed for Mayakovsky, Pasternak, Aseyev, and Tikhonov."[10]

We have already mentioned certain elements of vulgar sociology
in Bukharin's speech. In an address made by the young Communist
Youth proletarian poet, A. Bezymensky, it is not so much a question
of "certain elements" of sociology, but rather, one might say, a typical example of the RAPP way of thinking. Here is a short section
from it:

Before taking issue with Bukharin I wish to supplement his address and
speak about what he, unfortunately, didn't speak about. I think we should
refer not just to Soviet poets (in the direct and precise sense of that term)
but to those poets who provide a mouthpiece for the class enemy and also to
alien influences in the work of those poets who are near to us.

After indulging in passing references to "imperialist roman-
ticism" in Gumilyov and "kulak bohemianism" in Yesenin, as well as
to anti-Bolshevik and anti-city poems by Klyuyev, Klychkov, and
Chernov, Bezymensky then focused his attention on "the hidden
enemy."

The mask of nonsense which our enemy puts on is much more dangerous. This kind of work may be seen represented in the poetry of Zabolotsky,

a much underrated enemy. . . . In the guise of "infantilism" and deliberate nonsense Zabolotsky mocks us, and the genre corresponds exactly to the content of his verses and their ideas, while it is the "kingdom of emotions" which is disguised.

Bezymensky described another talented young poet, P. Vasilyev, as an overtly kulak poet:

Vasilyev's poetry for the most part ennobles and colorfully depicts a series of kulak figures, which stand in stark contrast to his portrayal of milk-and-water characters from our camp. His unconvincing abuse directed at the kulaks is more like a gentle reproach, and the actual figures evoke sympathy because of the savage strength with which the author invests them.[11]

These men were enemies; it is not without interest that both Zabolotsky and Vasilyev were arrested within a few years. But there were other poets who, according to Bezymensky, were being influenced by the enemies. Yaroslav Smelyakov, for instance, was "exposing himself not only to the influence of the bohemian and hooligan way of life, models of which are provided by Vasilyev's work . . . but to pernicious artistic influences as well." Moreover, "the influence of Zabolotsky can be seen at work in the productions of a poet as remarkable and as close to us as Prokofiev." After all this it was only too natural that Bezymensky should go on to overturn all that Bukharin had said about the poetry written by the representatives of proletarian literature who were far from out of date but who "had shown and would show again how Bolshevik they were and how youthful in creative terms."[12]

Demyan Bedny joined in the chorus of anti-Bukharin criticism in no uncertain terms. Bukharin had criticized Bedny more cautiously than Lenin (who had said that Bedny often followed the masses but never led them) and incomparably more gently than Stalin, who accused him of slandering the Soviet Union, of conceit, of debunking the proletariat of Russia and who responded to all the poet's objections by describing them as "the empty lamentations of a scared intellectual."[13] Nevertheless Bedny was not only mortally offended by Bukharin, he decided to make a public declaration of his sense of outrage at the Congress of Writers. The mere fact that Bukharin, when listing the truly outstanding Soviet poets, had linked Bedny's name with those of Mayakovsky and Yesenin, had offended him.

How do things stand (as far as his speech is concerned) with regard to myself? Bukharin has brought the corpse of Yesenin, stuck it on top of me and scattered Mayakovsky's ashes over the lot. Rest in peace! . . . Well, I've come out on to the platform especially to show you that I'm not dead yet![14]

Several times he referred to Pasternak either as a "lyrical nightingale" or a "grasshopper burbling something unintelligible in a disturbed and confused sort of language, something of a kind that he doesn't understand himself" and then proceeded to compare himself, clearly uninhibited by modesty, first with the Russian epic hero, Ilya Muromets, and then with an elephant.

In our outpost of heroic Russian poetry I am, of course, not Alyosha Popovich with his psaltery and his long tresses but, for want of a better comparison, I am Ilya Muromets full-grown. Aleksei Tolstoi's poem about him comes to mind. At the prince's feast Vladimir Fair-as-the-Sun left Ilya out of the toasting just as, at our congress, Bukharin has failed to drink my health . . . Ilya rode away frowning and muttering:

> . . . Without old Ilya, then,
> Let's see how you'll live!
> I'm worth more than them
> By putting women out of my mind
> And I can still bang my mace
> —I'm not a weakling yet!

. . . In all conscience I myself, listening to the lyrical nightingales, the unchallenged and traditionally acknowledged poets, realize that I do not belong to this breed, this avian breed. Lyric poets have nightingales' tongues. But I belong to the breed with strong teeth . . . I've got tusks. Old ones, cracked and jagged from honorable battles. But these tusks, let me assure you, are still strong, perhaps in one sense stronger than ever before. I've acquired some skill in using them and I never stop sharpening them.[15]

No more examples of the critical comments directed at Bukharin by other speakers need to be given, though there were many. In fact only one or two speakers voiced unqualified support, among them Yegishe Charents from Armenia and Sandro Euli from Georgia. Euli said this:

Bukharin's speech has given rise to a certain amount of passion which has somehow eclipsed the general joy prevailing at this congress. Some poets have replied and taken issue with him, striking attitudes which bear no relation to the state of literature today or tomorrow. Comrades, can we return to bygone stages in the development of our literature, say to the RAPP period? Can we rest on earlier achievements and be satisfied with them? We certainly cannot. . . . There must be and there can be no privileges, no allowances made on the basis of services rendered long ago. We must tolerate no grand old men and no well-meaning windbags in Soviet literature. Comrade Bukharin's speech calls us to a new, higher plane and I, representing the view of the Georgian delegation, express total solidarity with his speech.[16]

The acrimonious debate, full of emotion, charge and countercharge, which followed Bukharin's speech, clearly did more than excite him, it stung him to the quick. Winding up the discussion Bukharin, a brilliant debater, eschewed all academic and philosophical considerations of the nature of poetry and poetics. He made a striking, sharply critical speech, pointing out the errors, manipulations, and inaccuracies in his opponents' addresses.

Just as I expected, this congress has heard a series of vicious attacks upon my speech. I must apologize in advance to those comrades whom I shall challenge now as I wind up this debate, for I shall defend myself by all the rules of art. I must qualify my remarks in advance by saying that, unfortunately, the value of the arguments marshalled against me, in general cultural or narrowly specific terms, has not appeared to me to be of a particularly high order.[17]

And indeed Bukharin proceeded, by all the rules of art, to demonstrate beyond doubt the unscrupulous polemical tactics of Surkov, that "sharpshooter of the aggrieved faction," the unsubstantiated arguments of Kirsanov whose speech had been "a mine of information in the negative, logically, morally, and culturally," the primitively inept "conjuring tricks" of Bezymensky whose "conjurer's tackle stuck out from under his skirts." He ridiculed Demyan Bedny's self-advertisement: "It is a fine Ilya Muromets who, after a single, tiny critical remark, a diffident danger signal, turns into a dead body." He concluded with the following words:

Summing up the debate, I wish to state that the actual nature of the dissent between the two sides goes as follows. I am insisting on the essential need to use every effort toward raising the quality of our poetic production, embracing a titanic range of themes and bringing form to perfection—hence the slogan "learn and be venturesome!"; whereas my opponents, who are striving to present me as the annihilator of proletarian poetry, are resting on their laurels, losing ground, and, since they regard themselves as near-geniuses, are not exactly carried away by the problem of real, intense hard work. No other frontline of our culture has to put up with such strong individualism, such latter-day Oblomovitis often bordering on *arrogance*. Fear of tackling new problems, tranquility—these have now become typical. . . . Let us work together as friends to create the great poetry of socialism and do not complain if I have acted here as a weapon of straight-talking and logic. [18]

According to the shorthand report these concluding words were acclaimed by the delegates with "tumultuous applause." However, they were not actually the last words spoken. Bukharin's speech had been printed in advance and scanned by Stalin. A hint of this was given by Bukharin at the outset when he said that he considered the storm of applause which had greeted his appearance on the platform to be directed at that great Party "of which I am a member and which has entrusted me with the task of addressing this conference."[19] When Surkov came to speak against the basic principles formulated in that address he said significantly:

Comrade Bukharin stated in the introduction to his address that he had been entrusted to speak by the Party. I don't know what he meant by that. . . . At our congress all the speeches are delivered by the authority of the organizing committee. It appears to me that a speech is merely a starting point for discussion not a guiding principle apportioning light and shade in our poetry.[20]

This observation clearly reflected more than just Surkov's own personal opinion. Bukharin, however, not lacking experience in the realm of demagogic expression, refused to remain at a disadvantage. In the course of his winding-up speech he countered as follows:

Comrade Surkov seems to me to have adopted a dangerous political concept. He has said "the Party doesn't come into it, leave everything to the organizing committee." But is not the organizing committee controlled by the Party? This new concept therefore concerns a rift between our writers' organization and control by the Party. . . . At the beginning of my speech when the whole audience here had applauded me overgenerously, beyond my own merits, I stated that I considered this applause to be directed at the Party which had entrusted me with the task of addressing you. But Comrade Surkov started lecturing us in a different way—the Party doesn't come into it. I am nevertheless informed otherwise. The basis of my speech had been scrutinized by the proper authorities and its contents approved. This is one of the functions of Party control. . . . And no Comrade Surkov is going to sever the connection between our writers and Party control.[21]

These words also met with "prolonged applause" from the delegates. Bukharin's winding-up speech was interrupted twenty-seven times, according to the shorthand report, by "applause" or "laughter and applause." The undoubted success of this speaker clearly aroused the disapproval of those "proper authorities" who had scrutinized and approved the speech but not the winding-up address. This seems to be the likely explanation behind the fact that, before the Writers' Congress closed, Nikolai Bukharin read out the following brief announcement:

Since the harshness of my final speech has given rise to a number of misunderstandings and inquiries I consider it essential to declare that I was indeed overharsh in my statements and aggressive remarks directed at some of our poet-comrades, remarks intended to deal with a number of false accusations leveled against myself. I can, of course, in no way insist upon the justification of these harsh polemical expressions. If anyone has taken my words to mean that my assessment of individual writers as poets came to me in the form of obligatory directives, this is clearly a misunderstanding. Assessments of that kind cannot in any way be put on a level with political assessments. In the realm of poetry there must be wide-ranging freedom of competition in the search of creativity, in the setting of problems and their solution. Obligatory directives in this area would lead to a bureaucratization of the creative processes and would act as a disservice to the overall development of this artistic field. . . . In no way have I attempted, nor do I now attempt, to undermine the authority or discredit my opponents as poets and it has most certainly not been my wish to put the congress under that kind of pressure.[22]

The main idea behind this announcement was correct but its tone and character were such as to allow doubt to be cast before long over the entire content of Bukharin's speech and then his entire legacy as a literary critic. In any case the time was approaching when Stalin would have no further need of "strong-toothed" men like Bedny or Bukharin. Into the front rank were emerging other, younger writers, poets and leaders of the literary army whose teeth were sharper still.

The First Congress of Soviet Writers was a landmark in the history of Soviet literature. None of the five subsequent congresses was anything like so interesting as this first one. Virtually every single history of Soviet literature mentions this occasion. A few years ago the literary fraternity of the country organized a gala celebration of the fortieth anniversary of the first congress. Thus it is curious to note how Bukharin's speech and winding-up address are evaluated in our literary press *today*. As might be expected, we shall find no mention of the "hostile sortie" made by Bukharin at that congress, nor his "malicious slandering" of Soviet literature and poetry. Analyses of the events which occurred then either avoid all mention of Bukharin's name or else deal with him in a couple of unfair passing remarks. Even in the journal *Novy Mir* in a most engaging and substantial article written by A. Dementyev, "At the First Writers' Congress" and published under the editorship of Tvardovsky, this is what we find:

> Questions concerning artistic quality were posed by N. Bukharin in his address entitled, "On Poetry, Poetics and the Problems of Poetic Creativity in the USSR." However many conference delegates objected in principle to this speech, the point being that it contained unfair assessments of the work of several poets. Bukharin was particularly censured for his description of Demyan Bedny's poetry as out of date, his reduction of Mayakovsky's post-Revolution work to the level of elementary propaganda and his promotion of Pasternak and Selvinsky to the forefront of Soviet literature as models to be emulated, while keeping quiet about the contradictions inherent in their work.[23]

More or less the same comment appears in an article by A. Vinkel entitled, "Writers' Congresses in the USSR" which appears in the *Concise Literary Encyclopedia*:

> Many of the delegates objected in principle, and justifiably, to Bukharin's speech on Soviet poetry in which D. Bedny's poetry was declared out of date and Mayakovsky's post-Revolution work was reduced to mere propaganda.[24]

Although it is true that both Dementyev and Vinkel manage to avoid the usual clichés concerning "the line of rightist opportunism" adopted by Bukharin with regard to literature their reproaches are still quite unfair. This is easily demonstrated by turning once again to the text of his speech itself, from which we have already given quotations on Mayakovsky and Bedny. Take, for instance, what Bukharin said about Bedny:

Demyan Bedny is a true proletarian poet. [Applause] The underlying principle of his work is its mass appeal, its profound populism, its influence extending to millions. In this respect he occupies a quite unique position in the history of Soviet poetry. . . . Putting it in political terms we might speak of "a union between the working class and the peasantry under the hegemony of the proletariat." This is the ideological axle, the leitmotiv of his poetry; but the greatest breadth of its mass appeal is determined by the complexity of its creative components, and its material is drawn from everyday life.

The genres he uses are adjusted to the level of millions of readers: the song, the fable, the sharp comment, satire, narrative verse. There is nothing fanciful about his images; they are straightforward and yet incisive, understandable in real-life terms, drawn from the heart of life itself, containing the breath of life. The language inseparably associated with them is the sturdy language of the people, spoken by millions, direct and devastating, salted with proverbs and sayings, not far removed from folklore. . . . Its rhythms and the harmony of its lines are also profoundly popular which is why many of his verses have become folk songs enjoyed in town and village, in the army and navy, in city centers and the most remote outposts. His slightly crude, plain-man's humour with its sly subtlety, brings an involuntary smile to one's lips and his great fund of wholesome inner cheerfulness, strong as an oak, lends to his works, as they speed away swallowlike to every corner of this great country, the force of keen inspiration, of faith in the durability and invincibility of the Revolution. Sometimes Demyan rises to tremendous heights of general poetic applicability. . . . The works of Demyan Bedny are a living refutation of the prejudices against so-called tendentious poetry, once widely prevalent, notwithstanding Freiligrath, Heine, Barbier, and Béranger.[25]

Following all this, perhaps excessive, praise Bukharin made a single cautious, entirely justified remark criticizing Bedny. How can we write today that Bukharin "declared Bedny's poetry to be out of date"? He spoke of Mayakovsky as "the greatest and, from the poetic standpoint, the one innovatory figure in our poetry," a man who had become "a Soviet classic" whose works "would forever remain a remarkable poetic monument to a heroic age." He continued:

> This stormy, abrasive, enormous talent with a voice like thunder, has burst through to the proletariat with his tremendous fists . . . he has smashed a way through into the camp of proletarian poetry and taken up one of the foremost positions in it. . . . Everyone knows him. . . . Mayakovsky's poetry is profoundly relevant to actuality . . . it launches clouds of sharp arrows against the enemy, it is fire-spitting, all-consuming lava, it is a trumpet sounding on the field, calling us to battle.[26]

The brief survey of Mayakovsky's work which Bukharin made was constantly interrupted by applause from the delegates; in that section of the shorthand report alone there are two mentions of "applause," two of "tumultuous applause" and one which says "tumultuous applause; all stand." Of course Bukharin also referred to Mayakovsky's propaganda poetry, his agit-prop work at the time of the civil war. It was also natural that in a speech dealing with Soviet poetry as a whole he was unable to discuss every aspect of Mayakovsky's many-sided achievements. Nevertheless it would be entirely wrong to reproach him for having "reduced the whole of Mayakovsky's post-Revolution work to the level of elementary propaganda." Unfortunately even today it seems quite in order to misrepresent the ideas of Bukharin.

Seven

Nikolai Bukharin:
December 1934
to February 1936

THE SMALL AMOUNT OF liberalization occurring in politics and culture during 1935 extended also to the realm of economics. For the first time since 1928 the fall in agricultural productivity had been arrested and even turned into a slight rise; output for 1934 being five percent up on 1933. Requisitioning and purchase by the state also rose. The sale of foodstuffs in collective farm markets expanded. The export of grain was almost entirely stopped. Poverty, of course, remained the lot of a large proportion of collective farm workers but there was now no question of famine. Prospects for the 1935 harvest looked good and at the end of November the plenary session of the Party Central Committee passed a resolution to end rationing in the country's main industrial centers during the first quarter of 1935. Production of consumer goods for both town and country began to rise. The enormous industrial enterprises built during the First Five-Year Plan were increasing the output of industrial goods now that the millions of new workers who had entered the plants and factories for the first time had come to terms with their new situations and thus significantly improved the productivity of their labor. A slow economic recovery was now under way following the harsh, now irreversible social dislocations caused by the "revolution from above." There was every reason to anticipate that all of this would be accompanied by an extension of liberalization in political life.

Then, at this very time, Nikolayev's pistol-shot rang out in Leningrad.

Bukharin was shaken by the assassination of Kirov. Although the two of them had had many nasty quarrels in the past Bukharin regarded Kirov with affection and respect and Kirov returned the friendly feelings. In those years, it will be remembered, the Academy of Sciences was still located in Leningrad which meant that Bukharin often had to travel there and he even maintained a small flat in the city. If ever Bukharin was ill Kirov invariably visited him to take care of any necessary medical attention and to pass the time of day. Bukharin also visited Kirov's home. This is not to mention the fact that Kirov had been the initiator of that modest, almost unnoticed, liberalization which began after the Seventeenth Party Congress. Even before that congress he had become the second most important politician in the country and his popularity and influence were on the increase. The assassination of Kirov was certainly the most significant act of terrorism since the attempt on Lenin's life in 1918 and, whatever Bukharin may have thought about the motives behind the shooting in Smolny, he realized that the consequences of this event could prove to be far-reaching.

When the news of the murder broke in Moscow Bukharin was in the *Izvestiya* office. Ilya Ehrenburg recounts how, in the late evening of 1 December Bukharin dashed from room to room preparing the memorial edition. He apparently asked Ehrenburg to sit down straightaway and write an article about Kirov, but an hour or two later he is said to have called in again and exclaimed, "Don't write anything. It's a fishy business." This is clearly wrong testimony. Ehrenburg is perhaps recalling some subsequent conversation with Bukharin. Neither on 1 December nor during the days that followed could Bukharin have said the words attributed to him by Ehrenburg. In the memorial edition of the paper, 2 December, he himself wrote a long article about Kirov beginning as follows:

The news of Kirov's assassination has sent a sharp needle through the brain. Kirov has gone! That impassioned tribune with the sincere, ringing voice resonant of the great heart of the proletariat has gone. It is only a day or two since we all saw him at the plenary session of the Central Committee. There was his strong, sturdy figure, the firm handshake, the captivating voice arising from depths of tenderness. And that bold, modest, and yet enormous man now lies dead because some vermin have shot him dead, unarmed, at point-blank range, that man who went about everywhere like a rank-and-file working man, who spent days and nights in the factories and was unprecedentedly straightforward and approachable.

On 4 December, the day when the funeral train arrived in Moscow, Bukharin published another long article in *Izvestiya*, "Hello, Comrade Kirov," and on the day of the funeral, 6 December, yet another one, "Goodbye, Mironych."

In mid-December there came an announcement that the assassination of Kirov was the work of an underground organization of Zinoviev's followers in Leningrad. A group of men were arrested there; they were ex-supporters of Zinoviev, now declared accomplices of Nikolayev, and their leader was the hitherto virtually unknown I.I. Kotolynov. Zinoviev himself was arrested in Moscow, and shortly afterwards so was Kamenev; they were described as leaders of a certain "Moscow Center." At that time Bukharin could have had no reason to doubt this version. On 22 December an article by Bukharin, "Severe Words," was published in *Izvestiya*; it spoke of the responsibility devolved upon oppositional forces and said that any form of opposition which continues to insist on its mistaken ways was bound to turn into a counterrevolutionary organization. Thus Bukharin was, as it were, repeating Stalin's doctrine that any kind of opposition is a bad thing, that the opposition cannot be right since it remains in the minority and that the opposition has only two ways open to it: either the way of admitting that the Party is wholly in the right or the way of counterrevolution. Here is part of what he wrote.

Any "opposition" and any deviation ("left," "right," "rightist-ultra-left," "nationalist"), when it insists on pursuing its mistaken ways and continuing to fight, inevitably leads to a break in the Party, a break with Soviet legality, and to a counterrevolutionary function for the groups and people concerned. This is confirmed by the allegedly Fascist rebirth of such people as Trotsky and Zinoviev and their supporters who refused to lay down their arms.

This was clearly quite wrong; it was a purely Stalinist doctrine, and later on it would be used against Bukharin himself.

The fate of the so-called Leningrad Center is well known: all its members, held to be fully responsible for the assassination of Kirov, were subjected to a brief, secret trial and sentenced to be shot. All this occurred in December 1934; in January 1935 Zinoviev and Kamenev, along with a group of their erstwhile supporters, were sentenced to varying terms of imprisonment even though the court never established any facts which could be taken to prove their implication in the murder. At the same time a special session of the NKVD, without any court examination, handed down sentences of from two to five years' imprisonment to a number of once-prominent Party workers, ex-members of the "leftist" opposition, many of them well known to Bukharin.

Soon after the murder of Kirov and the sentencing of the Zino-viev- Kamenev group all Party organizations received a closed letter from the Central Committee giving a political evaluation of the events which had taken place. This was naturally remote from the truth. It laid stress on the notorious Stalin theory of the intensifica-tion of the class struggle as the building of socialism progressed. The letter gave not only hints but direct accusations against the former opposition which, as a spent force politically, was now turning to terrorism as a means of fighting against the Party and its leadership. Party members were urged to be particularly vigilant in relation to anyone who had once belonged to an opposition group. Although this concerned mainly members of the ex- "leftist" opposition, the ex-"rightists" also fell under suspicion. In any case among the con-siderable numbers of those arrested and sentenced "in connection with Kirov's murder" there were certainly some adherents to the "rightist" platform of 1928–29.

There can be little doubt that Nikolai Bukharin was one of the many people who sensed how the political atmosphere changed early in 1935 as compared with the latter half of 1934. The build-up of tension within the Party and outside was not a continuous process. The various kinds of danger signals were interspersed with events giving rise to hopes for a continuation of some sort of "liberalization." One such event was the Second All-Union Congress of Collective Farm Shock Workers in February. Bukharin was a speaker at that conference and his long speech was published in *Pravda* under the headline, "Collective Farmlands and Collective Farm People." The American historian, Stephen F. Cohen, suggests that Bukharin's speech at the collective farm-workers' conference was executed with "a very special tone." I disagree. The content of Bukharin's speech was no doubt more vivid and venturesome from the propaganda viewpoint than those delivered by many other speakers. It was not, however, particularly profound, and the speech contained quite a lot of the accepted clichés of the day, including praise addressed to "the great Stalin" who moved in good time to suppress all anti-Party deviation. However, Bukharin devoted part of his speech to the struggle against fascism and Hitlerism, the two threats not only to the country but to the entire world, which were apparent to Bukharin before many other politicians in the 1930s. His speech was also a further indication of his popularity, being interrupted several times by applause from the delegates. When he had finished Bukharin was given a prolonged standing ovation and people cheered. There is no doubt that, indirectly at least, Bukharin continued to play a much more important role in 1934–35 than his roles as editor of *Izvestiya* and candidate member of the Party Central Committee might suggest. Every one of his public utterances or articles (of which more will be said later) attracted wide attention. Nevertheless it would be quite wrong to seek in his every address some special hidden meaning and carefully disguised opposition to Stalin's policies.

We have already made passing reference to Bukharin's pamphlet criticizing the pope who had published a special anti-Bolshevik encyclical in the spring of 1929. G. Petrovsky described this as "a fine pamphlet" at the sixteenth Party Congress. In an up-to-date analysis of this work Stephen Cohen considers that Bukharin had managed to draw a fine analogy between the " 'corpse-like' obedience" and "unprincipled toadyism" imposed by the Jesuit Order of Loyola, and Stalinism. Cohen considers further that Bukharin's comments on the popes of Rome who reduced the Christians to a state of famine through their robbing and exploiting of their flock were actually addressed to Stalin rather than the pope. It is true that various forms of allegory, allusion, and transparent historical analogies, all the paraphernalia of so-called Aesopian language, have been used on a wide scale in political literature of all periods. The Bolsheviks themselves brought this to a fine art at one time. In his book *What Is to Be Done?* Lenin wrote:

> In a country ruled by an autocracy, in which the press is completely shackled, and in a period of intense political reaction in which even the tiniest outgrowth of political discontent and protest was suppressed, the theory of revolutionary Marxism suddenly forces its way into the censored literature, written in Aesopian language but understood by the "interested."[1]

Here Lenin has in mind the kind of allegorical references and analogies which are understood by those "interested." In Bukharin's articles and pronouncements during the period 1934–36, however, if there were any allusions and allegorical references they were so heavily disguised as to pass unnoticed by even those of his political adversaries who had an extremely keen interest in that kind of thing.

Let us return to the events occurring early in 1935. By the spring of that year the political tension—built up over the shooting by Nikolayev, the trials of Kotolynov and Zinoviev-Kamenev, the large-scale eviction of the "representatives" of the alien classes from Leningrad and Moscow, as well as a number of other acts of political terror—to all intents and purposes began to relax. In the principal cities rationing, the strict control over supplies of bread, meat and milk products, was brought to an end. This year was, in fact, the critical one for many branches of industry, the time when the success of industrialization became clearly established to the delight of the ordinary citizens and the rulers of the country alike. As if to arrange for all Soviet people to lose no time in forgetting the arduous, hungry years so recently passed Stalin spent 1935 setting up one campaign of mass propaganda after another. It was now that, at one of his receptions, he came out with the famous dictum "Comrades, life is better, life is more fun! And when life is good, work prospers." The Kremlin really did seem set to make life "more fun" with magnificent All-Union congresses and sumptuous receptions continually being arranged. The Second Congress of Collective Farm Shock Workers. The congress of leading stock-breeders. The Congress of Leaders in the Mechanization of Agriculture. The All-Union Congress of Stakhanovites. A grand reception for metal workers; another for workers in the gold industry. A grand reception for leading workers in the national economy and culture of the Georgian republic; the same for those of Armenia. Then an All-Union Conference for the *wives* of economic planners and engineer-technicians in heavy industry, followed by another for the *wives* of senior staff in the Red Army. Stalin attended all of these occasions in person along with members of the Politburo and the government. At many of them he read speeches, one to the Congress of Collective Farm Shock Workers, another at the reception for participants in the May Day Parade, another at the reception for builders and workers on the Moscow subway and another to the Stakhanovite Congress. He even addressed the leading men and women combine-harvester workers and the women shock-workers on collective farms producing beet. Another speech was given to leading collective farm workers from Tadzhikistan and Turkmenistan. Solemn ceremony in the Kremlin was followed by the setting of tables for thousands of people, and there at the head stood Stalin like a master of ceremonies. At no time before or afterwards did Stalin make so many welcoming speeches as in that year, 1935. On 4 May there in the Kremlin he was receiving and addressing graduates of the military academies. Once, during the informal part of the evening, Stalin, glass in hand, went suddenly over to Bukharin who was invited to every such occasion as editor of *Izvestiya*, and said, "I propose a toast to Comrade Bukharin. Our Bukharin, our old 'Bukharchik,' we all know him well and we love him. And anyone who rakes up the past can get out of here!"

At the end of the year the Seventh All-Union Congress of Soviets was held in Moscow. Agricultural, social, and political progress in the country was assessed and a decision was taken to draft a new

constitution for the USSR. Not only was Bukharin reelected to the
Union Council Central Executive Committee he was even appointed to the thirty-one-strong Constitution Commission which
had Stalin himself as chairman. Karl Radek was made chairman of
the Commission's subcommittee on the Electoral System and Bukharin headed the Legal Subcommittee which was given the task of
drafting the section concerning Soviet citizens' rights and obligations—the centerpiece of the new constitution.

Apart from the receptions organized for leading workers, shock
workers, and Stakhanovites in industry and agriculture, large-scale
propaganda campaigns were mounted in connection with the fifteenth anniversary of victory in the civil war, the fifteenth anniversary of the final defeat of Wrangel, and the fifteenth anniversary of
victory over the Polish interventionists. Practically every reception
or festival culminated in the mass awarding of orders of the USSR to
leading workers or veterans. People were decorated in their thousands and tens of thousands. Regions and republics were decorated
too. Most of the people's commissars, secretaries of regional committees, and heads of the republics were given the Order of Lenin.
The chairman of the Central Executive Committee, Abkhazi N.
Lakoba arrived in Moscow at the head of a delegation from his
republic and was invested with two orders in a single day, the Order
of Lenin for his successful work and the Order of the Red Banner for
active participation in the civil war in the Caucasus. Within a year,
however, Lakoba had been killed and posthumously declared "an
enemy of the people." And before many more years were out a lot of
the other regional and district leaders, commissars and department-
heads who were so liberally rewarded for their successful work in
1935 had fallen victims to repression.

This was a year in which Bukharin wrote dozens of substantial
articles and published them in his paper. We come across one or
two memoirs of the civil war and Revolution, several pieces devoted
to international issues and particularly the fight against fascism:
"Fascism and War," "The Problem of Peace," "Sergeant-Majors as
Voltaires, or the Philosophical Principles of National Socialism,"
and a series of his theoretical articles. "The Philosophy of a Cultured
Philistine" was directed against the famous Russian idealist philoso-

pher, Nikolai Berdyaev; "Do We Need a Marxist Science of History?" against certain erroneous ideas put about by the eminent Soviet historian, M. N. Pokrovsky. A number of these pieces have retained relevance and interest to this very day though they fall short of Bukharin's articles and pamphlets written in the 1920s. His sketches and articles on the problems of internal construction are by no means as rich or interesting in content. "On the Great Soviet Democracy," "Let Us Overturn the Norms," "How the World Will Be," "Our Union," "Man's Second Birth," "Socialism and the Population Policy"—these are more or less run-of-the-mill apologias lacking virtually any originality, independence of mind, profundity, or the usual Bukharin incisiveness and wit. Fairly often the tone is awful. For instance, writing on the prosperous life of collective farm workers, he claims that "the tractor of Stalin's policy is replowing our country" ("Reflections on the Tractor, etc." *Izvestiya*, 17 June 1935). Bukharin can hardly be blamed for this. Despite the fulsome toast proposed by Stalin, despite Bukharin's election to the Constitution Commission, there were plenty of people continuing to watch his every written or spoken word as he was well aware. A couple of minor inaccuracies in an article on friendship between children accompanying a selection of children's letters, and *Pravda* lost no time in bringing him into line.

On 2 February 1936 an *Izvestiya* leading article devoted to the triumph of the Leninist-Stalinist national policy claimed that now within the USSR the 'word "Russian" was spoken with pride and respect by peoples who in czarist times had equated it with the name of gendarme, priest, inflictor of punishment, or grasping merchant, in other words treated it as a noun generally denoting a political system which entailed famine, sickness, gradual death, and the extinction of national culture. The leader stopped short of anything criminal, of course; it contained nothing more than one or two journalistic exaggerations of the sort which appeared in virtually every political article of the period. However, a long editorial article in *Pravda* on 10 February included the following condemnation:

> Once again an *Izvestiya* leading article has resorted to a "universal" formula in the Bukharin manner which reflects the malicious slanders of all kinds of nationalists. It is the same tone that was adopted toward "the Rus-

sians" (in general) by nationalist groups in the Ukraine, Armenia, and Azerbaidzhan, by Georgian Mensheviks and Kazakhstan counterrevolutionaries and others.

On the anniversary of Lenin's death (21 January 1936) Bukharin had published an article in his paper which included these words.

Mensheviks were just what were needed—intolerant, steadfast, battle-hardened soldiers of revolution, her leaders men of steel who combined the latest in scientific theory with the latest in practical skill in order to turn the amorphous, uncomprehending masses in our country, where Oblomovitis was the prevailing characteristic, where a nation of Oblomovs was in power, into the shock troops of the world's proletariat.

Here, too, in the expression "a nation of Oblomovs" there was without doubt an element of journalistic exaggeration readily understandable to any intelligent reader. The article contained a number of other similar overstatements, such as references to Bolshevik leaders, "men of steel," etc. *Pravda*, however, in that same editorial article of 10 February, "Concerning a Putrid Concept" tore a strip off Bukharin, reminding him not only of the Decembrists, the Populists, Belinsky, and Chernyshevsky but even of Stenka Razin and Emelian Pugachev. One might have thought that the Russian nation had always been a model of revolutionary activity. The article said specifically:

The foolish and pernicious reactionary nonsense about the Russian people having been in the past nothing but a reactionary mass of lazybones and idlers, the incarnation of all-pervading Oblomovitis, Asiatic barbarism, and so on has been condemned by the Party more than once. It seems, however, that this putrid, slanderous "concept" is still alive and well. The ignominious role of giving it propaganda has fallen to Nikolai Bukharin. In *Izvestiya* on 21 January Comrade Bukharin writes about Russia as a country "where Oblomovitis was the prevailing characteristic, where a nation of Oblomovs was in power." According to him the people were nothing more than "amorphous, uncomprehending masses."

Conveniently forgetting what Chernyshevsky said about "a nation of slaves," which Lenin himself continually repeated, *Pravda* went on to quote from the latter's article on the national pride of the Great Russians and continued as follows:

Comrade Stalin has indicated with total exhaustiveness why Russia became the hearth of Leninism—but Bukharin still goes on about "a nation of Oblomovs." Has it never occurred to this author of this concept that his revelations are in implacable opposition to the whole history of our country, our Revolution and our Party? But what is mere history to Comrade Bukharin when he is overcome with a desire to set up a "new" universal formula? . . . Under the leadership of Stalin our country has been truly mighty and abundant, arising like a great gigantic crag of granite in the stormy waves of the capitalist world, delighting her friends with her success and striking down the enemy. Could this have been achieved by a "nation of Oblomovs"?

Only two days later, on 12 February 1936, an article by A. Leontyev devoted to a collection of speeches and articles by Stalin on the subject of the Ukraine included remarks to the effect that, "Quite recently Comrade Bukharin was guilty of a very serious mistake . . . coming out with a putrid concept and thus playing into the hands of the remnants of bourgeois-nationalist tendencies." Even though *Pravda*'s own articles contained much more in the way of journalistic overstatement than Bukharin's he had no alternative but to admit his mistake. He published a special clarification in *Izvestiya*, acknowledging how wrong he had been to refer to a "nation of Oblomovs," though he did affirm strongly at the same time that he had never entertained, and did not then entertain, any ideas which disclaimed the revolutionary services of the Russian people. It is easy to demonstrate, incidentally, that the expression "Oblomovitis" was a favorite phrase of Lenin's. Before the Revolution he often referred to the "semi-Oblomovitis" in Russia and he used the concept of Oblomovitis in relation to peasants and landowners, the Russian bourgeoisie, the Mensheviks and the Socialist Revolutionaries alike. Without ignoring the glorious past of the Russian people Lenin followed Chernyshevsky in using the abrasive journalistic expression "a nation of slaves." Following the triumph in October Lenin often wrote of "Oblomovitis" in regard to Soviet works and, yes, even the Bolsheviks. For instance, on one occasion he observed that "We have emulated the worst aspects of Czarist Russia, red tape and Oblomovitis, which are now literally choking us—the more sensible aspects we have not managed to emulate."[2] Elsewhere he wrote, "real, rampant irresponsibility is running wild, in our government departments and all their sections, and saboteurs are taking advantage of this: the result is Oblomovitis which is ruining everything."[3] He also wrote: "Russia has undergone three revolutions and Oblomovs still survive, since Oblomov was not only a landowner but also a peasant, and not only a peasant but also an intellectual, and not only an intellectual but also a Communist worker. You only have to watch the way we hold our meetings, the way we work in our commissions, *to be able to say that the old Oblomov has survived and that we must spend a lot of time washing, cleaning, gingering, and tousing him to get any sense out of him.* (Lenin's italics)[4] And again: "[We Bolsheviks] must make our brains more flexible and throw off all traces of Communist, or rather Russian, Oblomovitis and lots of other things."[5] In 1921, speaking not about Russia but about the Russian Federal Republic, Lenin claimed that throughout most of it the prevailing spirit was one of "rampant patriarchalism, Oblomovitis, semibarbarism and actual barbarism of the clearest kind."[6] Thus it might be said that there was no journalistic overstatement in the claim that the struggle against Oblomovitis in the Russian nation was one of the most important problems set for the Bolsheviks by Lenin. However, what Lenin was allowed to say Bukharin could not now be allowed to repeat.

Bukharin also published a string of articles outside the columns of his own newspaper. These included, for example, one for a collection about Michurin, an introduction to the Russian translation of Darwin's *The Origin of Species,* and a piece entitled *Living for Revolution* for another collection commemorating the fiftieth birthday of N. V. Krylenko, the people's commissar for justice. He paid close attention to the work of the Constitution Commission. The general range of his creative writing, however, narrowed perceptibly at this time and what was more important, his articles, speeches, and essays came to have less influence on the ideological life of the country than they had done a decade earlier. It seems clear that he was dismissed from all work in the Comintern; at all events there is no record of his participation in the Seventh Congress of the Comintern held in Moscow in July and August 1935 which was vital to the destiny of the worldwide Communist movement. Even though *Izvestiya*, naturally enough, gave detailed accounts of the progress of the conference it is quite possible that Bukharin, one time head of the Comintern, found it impossible to attend the meetings—even as a guest. A fair number of people who had once been close to Bukharin now avoided all contact with him, though this did not apply to Romain Rolland who arrived in Russia that very year.

In this period (1935) Bukharin continued to foster his own interest in literature and art but, more than that, he rallied to the defence of many people who were being subjected to tendentious criticism. For example, poems by Pavel Vasilyev and Nikolai Zabolotsky were published in *Izvestiya* despite the fact that these two authors had been branded as "enemies of socialism" by Bezymensky in a speech at the First Writers' Congress. Bukharin also used the columns of his paper to express support for the new production of the opera *The Queen of Spades* directed for the Leningrad Opera House by no less a talented figure than Meyerhold. Meyerhold had made substantial changes in the opera libretto originally written by Modest Tchaikovsky. The action had been transposed from the age of Catherine to Pushkin's own day, the 1830s. Although the *Izvestiya* reviewer observed that the new production did something of a disservice to Tchaikovsky, in that some of the scenes were omitted, he nevertheless concluded that in general this version of *The Queen of Spades* was "an event of the greatest significance in the history of the Soviet musical theater." This performance was one of "grand artistic scale, tremendous inventiveness on the producer's part, a high point in theatrical culture."[7]

Bukharin was doubtless aware that, for all the permanent holiday atmosphere, some kind of hidden and disturbing transformation was occurring within the Kremlin. V. Lominadze had committed suicide. V. I. Nevsky, the distinguished Party historian and oldest of Bolsheviks, head of the State Public Library, had been arrested. Following the arrest of a number of Central Executive Committee staff members, A. Yenukidze, its permanent secretary, a man considered to be a friend of Stalin's, was accused of failure to maintain necessary vigilance and of social sabotage." At the plenary session of the Central Committee he was sacked and expelled from the Party. All these events were a source of great concern to Bukharin.

The year 1934 witnessed great changes also in Bukharin's personal life. Earlier, in 1929 or 1930, he had been divorced from his second wife E. I. Gurvich, an economist, by whom he had had a daughter called Svetlana. (His first wife had been Nadezhda Lukina, the sister of an Old Bolshevik, Nikolai Lukin, a scholar, historian, and member of the Academy). In the 1920s both marriage and divorce were comparatively simple matters at least as far as formalities were concerned. Most Bolsheviks never bothered to register their marriages—they simply came together and lived with each other. When children came along families grew up which were conceivably more closely knit than nowadays. There were, of course, occasions when these families fell apart, in which case the people concerned simply separated, the children normally remaining with the mother. The question of dividing up property seldom arose because the Bolsheviks of that period had very little in the way of "personal belongings." Getting divorced from E. Gurvich was high drama for Bukharin, even though their marriage had never been solemnized and they had in fact lived most of the time in separate flats, Bukharin with his father in the Kremlin, Gurvich with their daughter in her Moscow apartment. Bukharin married his third wife in 1934; she was Anna Mikhaylovna Larina, a beautiful young woman of nineteen. In 1935 she moved in with him and they began living together, though without registering the marriage. Anna came from a family of professional revolutionaries. She was the daughter of a well-known party activist, Yu. Larin (Mikhail Aleksandrovich Lourié) who had joined the Social Democrats in 1901 at the age of nineteen. A Menshevik in 1904 (in exile) he transferred allegiance to the Bolshevik party in August 1917. At that time Lenin looked upon ex-Mensheviks with the greatest suspicion. Differences in party allegiance in Russia often signified not just policy differences but differences in temperament, character, and personality-type. The Mensheviks tended to attract people of moderate inclinations, with a sense of compromise, people who, although lacking in revolutionary initiative, nevertheless adhered more strictly to the dogma of ninteenth-century Marxism. The Social Revolutionaries drew upon young people without much taste for the theory of revolution but with a thirst for swift and effective revolutionary action (individual terror). They could not be bothered with the establishment of a strong, centralized organization and thus, like the Mensheviks, they were short on discipline and cohesion. This was why Lenin strove to limit the flow of converts from other parties into the ranks of the Bolsheviks. He personally had Larin's name removed from the list of Bolshevik candidates up for election to the Constituent Assembly in 1917, though relations between the two of them were to undergo a subsequent change. In 1918–19 Larin worked very conscientiously at the establishment of a Soviet system of finance and produced a whole series of enactments on economic affairs. He was one of the founding members of the State Planning Commission, Gosplan. He supervised the nationalization of trade, the creation of the first state farms, and the canceling of Czarist loans. It would be no exaggeration to describe Larin as one of the most prominent creators of the economic system known as "war communism." And this was the period during which Bukharin drew even nearer to the Larin family which he had come to know closely ever since the time of their emigration during World War I.

At the onset of NEP the part played by Larin in the formulation of Soviet economic policy diminished though even then he continued to help work out important details concerning the monopoly of foreign trade, the policy on concessions, etc. Just when Bukharin came out as an immediate and active proponent of NEP Larin, up until 1924, spoke out against its extension since he regarded the policy as the retreat of the proletariat. In 1922–23 he was insisting on the curtailment of concessions made to the private trader and making references to the need for "Communist reaction," for the elimination once and for all of private capital from trading, for the orientation of rural policy toward the poor peasant and the small-time middle peasant, etc. By 1925 he had come round to a truer understanding of the essential meaning of NEP and begun to participate in the resolution of many economic problems. Now, however, he was a very sick man suffering from progressive muscular dystrophy.

He died in 1932, aged 49, and was given a state funeral in Red Square.

Larin's wife was the sister of the wife of V. P. Miliutin, the prominent Bolshevik writer and economist and a friend of Bukharin's. In the late 1920s Miliutin—the first people's commissar for agriculture—was director of the Central Statistical Board, a member of the Labor and Defence Council, the Council of People's Commissars and the Central Executive Committee, and the author of a number of works on agrarian policy and world economy.

Anna Larina, therefore, was familiar from childhood with most of the prominent Party figures of the time. She was particularly close to Bukharin who often visited his colleagues and comrades both in the Kremlin and in the government "house on the embankment" where he loved playing games with the children. She became his wife and went to live with him when he was forty-five. His Kremlin flat had been occupied by Stalin until 1932 but, following the suicide of Nadezhda Alliluyeva, Stalin had asked him to exchange rooms because it was painful for him to continue living there. Stalin also knew Anna Larina and when he heard of the marriage he rang up to congratulate her. One day soon afterwards he met Bukharin with his wife in the Kremlin and said to him, "Nikolai, you've outgalloped me again."

Eight

Abroad

NIKOLAI BUKHARIN OFTEN WENT ABROAD. Before the Revolution when he was arrested in 1910, following the collapse of the whole Moscow party organization and threatened with a vicious sentence, years of penal servitude and hard labor, he managed to escape from captivity and flee the country. In emigration he visited France, Sweden, Switzerland, Austria, Norway and contributed actively both to the Russian émigré press and that of the Western European socialists. He studied a good deal in various libraries, particularly Marxism and political economy. He was abroad when he first got to know Lenin, in Cracow in the autumn of 1912. The following year he first met Stalin in Vienna. The latter had come to that city in January with several assignments from Lenin, the most significant one being the completion of his pamphlet *Marxism and the National Question* in which, as is well known, he devotes a lot of space to criticizing the nationalist policy of the Austrian Social Democrats. Stalin did not speak German, however, and it fell to Bukharin to help him out over a period of days with this work which was published shortly afterwards in the Russian journal *Enlightment*. This was the piece which established Stalin's reputation as an expert on the nationalist question and this in turn was the reason for his nomination in 1917 as people's commissar for the affairs of the nationalities.

In the 1920s Bukharin's work for the Comintern frequently took him abroad and in 1931 he visited London to attend an international congress on the history of science. Now again, in 1936, the question arose of Bukharin paying another visit to the countries of Western Europe. It was probably at the end of 1935 that the inner circles of the Party Central Committee raised the possibility of the Soviet government purchasing sections of the Marx and Engels archives from the German Social Democrats. These people were in urgent need of funds and were prepared to sell some of the classic documents of Marxism to the Soviet Union, though they would naturally retain copies. Was there anyone more suited to the task of conducting these negotiations than Nikolai Bukharin? In any event, on Stalin's initiative he was nominated leader of a group whose purpose was to familiarize itself with the Marx and Engels documents and look into the possibility of purchase. The group also included A. Ya. Arosev, a forty-six-year-old Bolshevik writer who had earlier been a professional revolutionary, taken part in underground Party activities and, during the years of civil war, occupied responsible military positions. By 1936 he had become head of VOKS, the All-Union Society for Cultural Relations with Foreign Countries. Another member of the group was V. V. Adoratsky, the director of the Marx-Engels-Lenin Institute, not the brightest of men but one who had begun to display increasing activity "on the ideological front" in the 1930s. There were, of course, other people in the group, less well known but perhaps no less influential in the negotiations.

The Politburo resolution also named the persons whom Bukharin was to meet and with whom he should conduct negotiations. One of them was Léon Blum, leader of the French Socialists, and another was Otto Bauer, the Austrian Social Democratic leader renowned for his theoretical contribution to that current of Marxist thinking known as "Austro-Marxism." Some of the Russian Mensheviks were earmarked as go-betweens in the forthcoming negotiations. Central among them was Boris I. Nicolaevsky, a fifty-year-old journalist, author, and historian, personally responsible for collecting while abroad a voluminous and valuable archive on the history of the Social Democratic movement in Russia. The leader of the Russian Mensheviks, Fyodor I. Dan, who had been head of the Central Executive Committee of the Soviets in 1917, was also picked out. Nicolaevsky had emigrated from Soviet Russia in 1921; Dan had lived on there into 1922 but had then been deported as "an enemy of the Soviet state." Bukharin knew the Social Democrats named in the Politburo resolution though he could scarcely have met Dan or Nicolaevsky since the October Revolution.

Bukharin accepted the Politburo assignment and prepared for the journey abroad with some anxiety and care. Naturally in the past, notwithstanding the bitter political polemics between them, the Bolsheviks and Social Democrats had arranged several deals aimed at the acquisition of copies taken from the works of Marx, Engels, and their closest disciples. Foremost among the organizers of these was David B. Riazanov, the leading Bolshevik expert on the works of Marx and Engels. Before the Revolution he had researched widely in the archives of the German Social Democratic party and published a number of valuable works on Marxist ideology, such as *Anglo-Russian Relations in the Evaluation of Marx* and *Karl Marx and the Russian People of the Forties*. Riazanov was anything but dogmatic in his views, and his critical comments on Marx's attitude to the historical development of Russia and czarist foreign policy were most convincing. Shortly after the October Revolution the Party entrusted him with the task of setting up the Institute of K. Marx and F. Engels with himself as director. This was the institute which began preparation of the first academic edition of the complete works of Marx and Engels.[1] In the early 1920s Riazanov adopted an extremely negative attitude to Stalin and did not seek to hide it. Stalin, not surprisingly, was biding his time before dealing with him. The right moment presented itself during the falsified trial of the so-called Union Bureau of Social Democratic Mensheviks. The investigators forced one of the accused men, I. I. Rubin, to testify that all the basic documents of this entirely nonexistent organization were deposited with Riazanov in his institute. Immediately following the evidence given by Rubin the organs of the GPU dispatched a large task force to the Marx and Engels Institute in order to carry out a search. Riazanov, as director, refused to allow the security men into his offices or storerooms, stating simply that the Party had entrusted him with safeguarding the legacy of Marx and Engels and he was not going to allow the Security Police to dig about among such priceless materials. The leader of the GPU task force rang the Central Committee and received instructions to go ahead with the search and place Riazanov under house arrest. The search went on for several days. Naturally no file of documents relating to the "Union Bureau" was ever found. They did find a large file of documents of the Trotskyite faction which Karl Radek had handed to Riazanov for safekeeping. As a scholar Riazanov could not bring himself to refuse to look after any materials connected with the history of the Bolshevik party. Karl Radek suffered no punishment at that time, but Riazanov was sacked from his post as director of the institute and expelled from the Party for his "direct assistance of Menshevik interventionists and betrayal of the Party." Soon afterwards he was banished from Moscow.

In previous years Bukharin and Riazanov had been close friends. Each had been a prominent theoretician of Marxism and a full member of the USSR Academy of Sciences. Now here was Bukharin, about to continue the very work which Riazanov had carried out before. I am not aware of any mention in the Soviet press of the setting up of Bukharin's group, or its terms of reference. Nor did Bukharin write anything on the subject for his paper from abroad, though the Western press published a fair number of varying reports. The group passed swiftly through Vienna, Berlin, Amsterdam, and Copenhagen before settling for a long stay in Paris where Bukharin, Arosev, and Adoratsky occupied adjoining rooms in the *Lutetia*, one of the finest hotels in the city. Bukharin's wife soon joined him there and the two of them saw the sights of Paris. Some of the sightseeing was conducted without her since Anna was in the eighth month of pregnancy.

Bukharin met not only Nicolaevsky and Dan while he was in Paris, but also a number of the country's cultural figures such as André Malraux. The leader of France's Socialist party, Léon Blum, soon to become head of the Popular Front government in France, gave a luncheon party in honor of Bukharin and the Soviet delegation. On 3 April 1936 Bukharin read a long paper at a conference of the Paris Association for the Study of Soviet Culture entitled "Fundamental Problems of Contemporary Culture." The large audience applauded the speaker with enthusiasm and soon afterwards the speech was published in Paris in pamphlet form.

Ilya Ehrenburg, a close friend of Bukharin's, was another person whom he met frequently at this time. They had become friends years before in childhood, studying together at the same high school. During the first Russian Revolution the two of them had taken part together in the organization of public meetings and strikes. Ehrenburg soon became a professional writer while Bukharin became a professional revolutionary, though they maintained close contacts. When Bukharin took over the editorship of *Izvestiya* he asked Ehrenburg to remain the paper's permanent correspondent in Paris where the writer spent most of his time, and Ehrenburg agreed. In the mid-sixties, when talking to me about Stalin, Ilya Ehrenburg spoke fondly of Bukharin as a close friend. He told me that Bukharin had willingly consented to travel to Paris, though not without misgivings. "I don't know," he is said to have commented, "perhaps it's a trap." However, I found out later that Ehrenburg was far from one hundred percent accurate in his testimony; he frequently mixed up dates and places.

Bukharin's mission to Paris soon ground to a halt. The purchase of the archives did not take place, Stalin having discovered that the German Social Democrats were demanding too high a price for the documents in question. Bukharin, who reported regularly back to Stalin on the progress of the negotiations ("Koba loves receiving letters" he said to Ehrenburg), broke off the negotiations and flew back to Moscow with his wife. They arrived home on May Day 1936 and eight days later Anna gave birth to a son whom they called Yuri.

Bukharin's journey abroad is referred to in many subsequent memoirs and historical researches. André Malraux, Nicolaevsky, Dan's widow, and many others have written about their conversations with Bukharin. One specific point which emerges from their reminiscences is that Bukharin discussed with several people the question of whether he should or should not return to the USSR. He seems to have been convinced that it would not be long before Stalin had him eliminated. He would say things like, "He'll finish us all off," "He's Satan," or "We're all doomed." In the 1960s Lydia

Dan described Bukharin coming to their house late one night in a very agitated frame of mind and spending hours in conversation with her late husband. Bukharin appears to have spoken frankly to Dan of the state of affairs in the Central Committee and predicted both the widespread terror and his own destruction. He stated openly that Stalin was incapable of abstaining from vengeance; any Communist at all favored by the Party or simply more capable or better informed than Stalin inevitably provoked in him both fear and anger. Stalin had nevertheless become the symbol of socialism, this was a fait accompli and nothing could be done about it. When Dan had begun to entreat Bukharin to stay on in France, the latter had said it was not possible. "I cannot live in emigration. I must go back and drain my cup to the dregs."

It is my belief that these reminiscences contain a fair proportion of conjecture. Many conversations which took place in Dan's house *about* Bukharin have now become conversations *with* Bukharin. What is established fact is that Bukharin was extremely cautious in his dealings with the Mensheviks and the leaders of the Western socialists. Whenever one of them called on him at the hotel Bukharin would always ask them to wait a minute and would then slip next door to invite Adoratsky and Arosev in to join them in conversation. Bukharin's activity and movements were under secret surveillance by the French police who feared an attack on him by one of the many different Russia White émigré groups living in Paris. On one occasion the police were reliably tipped off about a proposed attempt on Bukharin's life and for two solid days the Hotel *Lutetia* was cordoned off by them. Shortly after this incident Bukharin transferred to the Soviet embassy and remained there until the end of his mission. In addition to this there is little doubt that NKVD agents specially sent to Paris were also observing Bukharin's behaviour. It is therefore hardly proper to think in terms of Bukharin wandering about freely all over Paris.

Some months after Bukharin had left Paris the chief organ of the Menshevik émigré press, *Socialist Herald* (*Sotsialisticheskiy vestnik*), which came out every two weeks under Dan's editorship, published anonymously a "Letter of an Old Bolshevik" (No. 23/24,

1936). This was continued in issues No. 1 and 2 for 1937. At the time this document evoked much comment and opinion. Many people attributed this "Letter" to Bukharin himself, an Old Bolshevik and a recent visitor to Paris who had had many meetings with the editor of the paper. I have had occasion to comment on this "Letter of an Old Bolshevik" before.[2] It is a document which suggests that the author was extremely well informed of such recondite matters as the Ryutin affair, the relationship between Stalin and Kirov, the assassination of Kirov and its aftermath, the first trial of Zinoviev and Kamenev, and other such matters. Many of the events referred to (the death of Gorky, the second trial of Zinoviev and Kamenev, the removal of Yagoda and his replacement by Yezhov, etc.) took place, however, after Bukharin's departure from Paris. Besides which the document in question contains a number of inaccuracies which Bukharin could scarcely have perpetrated. The roles of Yezhov, Stetsky, and Arganov are clearly exaggerated. The author claims that Yezhov replaced the whole leadership of the NKVD with the exception of Arganov. What actually happened is that Arganov was himself arrested soon after Yagoda and Yezhov won over Zakovsky, Frinovsky, Redens, Kedrov, and many other ex-assistants of Yagoda. L. Sosnovsky was merely expelled from the Party and arrested in 1936; it was a whole year before he died. These errors and one or two other details betray the *foreign* authorship of the "Letter of an Old Bolshevik." In the 1930s there were no centers of Sovietology in Western countries such as have sprung up since World War II. Information concerning events in the "upper strata" of the Soviet Union ("Kremlinology") was available, however, and it was collected with scrupulous care in two centers, in the circles of *Socialist Herald* and around Trotsky who was currently publishing his "Bulletin of the Opposition." The "Letter of an Old Bolshevik" has the air of a careful compilation of many different rumors and reports which had leaked out through various channels to the West.

I gave it as my own opinion that this "Letter" was composed by Nicolaevsky without knowing that he had already openly claimed authorship. Shortly before his death in the USA (in 1966) Nicolaevsky published a book in English entitled *Power and the Soviet*

Élite in which he included the "Letter of an Old Bolshevik" together with a number of other essays. The American editor of his book, Janet D. Zagoria, had interviewed the seventy-eight-year-old author and the main theme of the interview was a seies of meetings between Nicolaevsky and Bukharin in Paris in 1936. There is a distinct possibility some inaccuracies have crept into the interview. Nicolaevsky does seem to have been not only summarizing several conversations between himself and Bukharin but also bringing in information culled from other sources. Nevertheless it is worth quoting an extract from the interview: here the conversation concerns the relationship between Bukharin and Lenin.

INTERVIEWER: Did you discuss any people with Bukharin—Lenin, Stalin or others?

NICOLAEVSKY: Yes. His remarks about Lenin were particularly interesting too, because Bukharin was so devoted to him. Even when he spoke about their disagreements—over the Malinovsky case, for example—he did so in a tone of warmth and friendship.

This is what he told me about the final period of Lenin's illness. From various details in Bukharin's account, I gathered that he meant the early fall of 1922. "Lenin would summon me to come and see him," Bukharin said. "The doctors had forbidden him to speak lest he become upset. But when I arrived, he would immediately take me by the hand and lead me into the garden. He would begin to speak: 'They don't want me to think about this. They say that this upsets me. But why don't they understand that I have lived my whole life this way? If I cannot speak about this, I become more upset than when I do speak. I calm down when I am able to talk about these matters with people like you.'"

I asked Bukharin what the conversations had been about. He replied that he and Lenin spoke mostly about "leaderology," as we called it—that is, the problem of succession, of who was fit to be leader of the Party after Lenin was gone. "This," said Bukharin, "is what worried and upset Lenin the most."

In this connection, he told me that the last articles of Lenin's, *Better Less but Better*, about cooperatives and so forth, were only part of what Lenin had planned to do. He had wanted to put out another series of approximately the same number of articles which would give a complete picture of the future policy to be pursued. This was his principal goal.

Lenin's testament consisted of two parts, a small part about the leaders, and a bigger one about policies. I asked Bukharin what the principle of

Lenin's policy was. He said to me: "I have written two things about this policy, *The Road to Socialism and the Worker-Peasant Alliance* and *Lenin's Political Testament*. The first is a pamphlet, which came out in 1925, the second was published in 1929." Bukharin asked me, "Do you remember those pamphlets?" I replied, "I confess I don't at present remember *The Road to Socialism*."

"That is the more interesting one," he said. "When I wrote it, I included my conversation with Lenin about the articles already published and those not yet published. I tried in that pamphlet to keep to only what Lenin thought, of what he told me. Of course, they were not quotations; my understanding of what he meant was reflected in what I wrote. But it was my outline of Lenin's ideas as he expounded them to me. The main point of his testament was that it is possible to arrive at Socialism without applying more force against the peasantry." The question concerned, of course, the treatment of the peasantry, which constituted 80 per cent of the population of Russia. In the opinion of Lenin and of all Communists in general, it was possible to apply force against the peasantry at a given moment, yet this was not to be made a permanent method of treatment. This was the point of *The Road to Socialism*.

With *Lenin's Political Testament*, Bukharin said, it was a different matter. "There were big arguments about it, and I had to write only about what Lenin had already published. It was fundamentally the same thing. But the first pamphlet went further and the ideas in it were more crystallized; it did not stop at what he had already written."

I have reread these pamphlets and I see that Bukharin was quite right in presenting Lenin's ideas in this way. This was the way Lenin thought. And Lenin considered Bukharin the one most able to convey his thoughts. He spoke with him so that Bukharin would write what he himself had left unsaid.[3]

Western experts on Soviet affairs accept Nicolaevsky's statements as authentic, at least as far as this conversation with Bukharin is concerned. Although all reminiscences, and especially those recalling conversations which took place as long as thirty years previously, are prone to a certain amount of inaccuracy, in the present instance my inclination is to consider Nicolaevsky's testimony to be reliable. Bukharin was aware that Nicolaevsky was engaged in an exhaustive study of the history of the Social Democratic movement, including that of Bolshevism, and there was no reason to withhold important facts concerning the last months of Lenin's life.

Nine

The Difficult Summer and Arduous Autumn of 1936

———— »» «« ————

BACK HOME AGAIN IN Moscow Bukharin returned to his work on *Izvestiya* and on the Central Executive Committee Commission on the Constitution. On 12 June 1936 the new constitution was published in draft form and discussion of it began. On 14 and 15 June Bukharin published in his paper a long article analyzing and elucidating the section of the constitution relating to the rights and obligations of Soviet citizens. Maxim Gorky died in Moscow on 18 June and, having been on good terms with him for many years, Bukharin wrote several articles on the writer during the period of mourning culminating in "The Last Farewell" published in *Izvestiya* on the day of the funeral. On 6 July he published "The Routes of History: Thinking Aloud," the last of his articles to appear in *Izvestiya* and probably one of the last that he ever wrote. It touched directly upon the rise of fascism and some commentators (Cohen, for example) believe that Bukharin used this article as a disguise for the expression of his misgivings about the tightening of the regime in the USSR.

In mid-July Bukharin took a holiday which he decided to spend as far away from Moscow as possible. Lenin is known to have enjoyed hunting and often went on trips for two or three days in the forests just outside Moscow in order to wind down when suffering from overwork. Many Bolshevik leaders of the time followed

Lenin's example and turned to hunting as a favorite form of relaxation. Trotsky was one of them. Stalin went hunting from time to time often taking along the old writer Mikhail Prishvin, a committed veteran hunter. Sometimes he also invited another writer, Boris Pilnyak, whose story "The Tale of the Unextinguished Moon" (on the death of the civil-war hero, General Frunze), written in 1925, had angered him. Pilnyak had hinted that Stalin had been guilty of bungling the medical attention given to the army commander. The issue of *Novy Mir* which contained Pilnyak's tale was soon removed from sale and reclaimed from subscribers. By the late 1920s, however, Stalin seems to have "forgiven" Pilnyak. Bukharin also liked hunting and on this occasion he decided to go down to Kirghizia and relax in the Pamir region. One of his secretaries traveled with him and it is quite possible that this man had been instructed to keep a watch on Bukharin.

Once in Frunze Bukharin soon hired local guides and left for the mountains. In those days there were no such things as transistor receivers and he heard no news. Meanwhile on 19 August in the Moscow House of Unions there began the retrial of Zinoviev, Kamenev, and a number of their supporters, accused now no longer merely of "moral responsibility" for the assassination of Kirov but of the direct organization of this act of terrorism and many other crimes, such as conspiracy to murder the whole of the Politburo. Some of the accused, including Zinoviev himself, went beyond their "testimony" given at the preliminary hearing and suddenly began giving evidence of their "criminal" contacts with Bukharin, Rykov, Tomsky among the ex-rightists in opposition, and also with Radek, Piatakov, Sokolnikov, Serebriakov, and other ex-Trotskyites, even with Shliapnikov, the leader of the so-called workers opposition in 1921. All of these people were still free as the new trial began. Radek even wrote a long article "The Trotskyite-Zinoviev Gang of Fascists and Its Leader, Trotsky" which was published in *Izvestiya* on 21 August. In the very same issue on another page part of the testimony given by Kamenev reads as follows:

> In 1932–34 I personally maintained contacts with Tomsky and Bukharin and kept myself informed of their political attitudes. They sympathized

with us. When I asked Tomsky about Rykov's attitude he replied, "He thinks as I do." Asked about Bukharin he said, "He thinks as I do but his tactics are different. He disagrees with the Party line but his tactical approach is one of strengthening his infiltration into the Party and gaining the personal confidence of the leadership."

This was accompanied by evidence from Zinoviev which included compromising material on Shliapnikov, Lominadze, Shatsky, Smilga, and Sokolnikov, and further evidence from others incriminating Radek. Needless to say, no further articles by Radek ever appeared again in *Izvestiya* or any other newspaper.

Next day all the papers printed a special announcement by the USSR public prosecutor and prosecutor at the current trial, A. Vyshinsky. It included this paragraph:

At previous hearings some of the accused have given evidence describing Tomsky, Bukharin, Rykov, Radek, Piatakov, Serebriakov, and Sokolnikov as persons participating to a greater or lesser extent in criminal activities. I consider it necessary to inform the court that yesterday I issued instructions for investigations to begin into the accusations made by the accused with regard to Tomsky, Rykov, Uglanov, Bukharin, Radek, and Piatakov. Depending upon the outcome of these investigations by the public prosecutor's office justice shall take its course in this case. With regard to Serebriakov and Sokolnikov our investigation agencies are already in possession of facts which testify that these persons stand revealed as having participated in counterrevolutionary activities, in connection with which criminal proceedings are being brought against Sokolnikov and Serebriakov.

It may be supposed that Sokolnikov and Serebriakov were arrested before the trial began. Lominadze was already dead. Smilga, Shliapnikov, and Shatskin seem also to have been taken into custody.

From 19 August 1936 onwards all over the country mass meetings were held in works and institutions at which people clamored for those who had betrayed the country to be severely punished. On 20 and 21 August the newspapers began publishing resolutions passed by many meetings demanding "an exhaustive inquiry into the links between Bukharin, Rykov, and Tomsky with the criminal Trotskyite-Zinoviev gang." These demands were published in the columns of *Izvestiya* and reprinted in the leading article of the newspaper which bore as usual on the back page the legend "Editor: N. I. Bukharin."

Meanwhile Bukharin himself was far away from Moscow in the Pamir mountains. However, soon after the start of the trial Bukharin's companion fell ill (or pretended to) and Bukharin began to ride back down to Frunze. There he too learned of the trial from the newspapers. He was thunderstruck by what he read. Before this he had been broken psychologically, aware as he was that certain dangerous processes were under way and that the successes achieved in the building of socialism were matched with various emerging symptoms of degeneration in the regime. But he had dispelled these ideas and continued to fulfill everything asked of him by Stalin and the Politburo with conscientious loyalty. He had accepted the first trial in the case of Zinoviev and Kamenev as a necessary evil. Kirov had, after all, been assassinated by Zinoviev's men. He could even believe that the inquiry had now unearthed some new circumstances and that Kamenev and Zinoviev were guilty of much more than had been apparent eighteen months before. Bukharin had known Yagoda and his closest assistants for years and he simply could not imagine they were obtaining confessions through intimidation and torture. Now, as he read the evidence of the two men, Bukharin came to the conclusion that they were consciously naming ex-members of the opposition—himself included—in order to sully the lot of them.

Bukharin came back down into Frunze on either the last or the penultimate day of the trial. As well as the Moscow papers, which arrived in Frunze a day or two late, the local press was also reporting the trial. Immediately Bukharin sent an urgent telegram to Stalin asking him to delay carrying out the sentence (he had no doubt that they would be sentenced to be shot). He wanted to arrange a confrontation with the accused so that he, Bukharin, could refute the allegations leveled at him. It seems that he was still there in Frunze when he learned that the sentence had been carried out.

He now expected to be arrested in Frunze but it did not happen. Leaving all his things behind in Kirghizia he took the first plane

back to Moscow. In those days even by air the journey took no less
than twenty-four hours. Next day someone telephoned Anna and
told her to go and meet her husband. She too had spent all these
days in anxious uncertainty, receiving no letters, every day reading
the newspapers full of allegations made by the accused against her
husband, allegations which she simply could not believe. She now
took the car assigned to Bukharin (the chauffeur being a man who
was very fond of Nikolai Ivanovich) and drove out to the airport
which was then located where the present subway station "Aero-
port" stands, on the far side of the Leningrad Highway. They were a
few minutes late. Bukharin had already flown in and was sitting in a
corner of the hall with his face buried in his hands (so that he would
not be recognized). Anna and the chauffeur went up to him. "Hello,
Nikolai. Come along home." "Where?" "Home. To the Kremlin."
"Will they let us in?" "They will as long as we live there." "All right,
but hide me. I don't want people to see me," said Bukharin and
went off to the car.

The first thing Bukharin did when he got home was to ring
Stalin. But Stalin was not in Moscow. Once the trial and execution
were over he had gone down to Sochi "for a rest." Bukharin wrote
him a long, detailed letter and then never went out for several days.
No one rang him either. No one called. Discussing the trial with his
wife he assured her that he was guilty of nothing. The young woman
was finding it hard to believe in Zinoviev's guilt. She asked her husband, "What do you think—could Zinoviev and Kamenev have
killed Kirov?" "Well, they're killing me with their evidence," was
Bukharin's answer.

Bukharin was also shocked by Tomsky's suicide. He did not
know the circumstances under which this had been carried out, did
not know that Stalin had visited Tomsky in his flat, that they had
spoken face to face, and that Stalin had arrived with a bottle of wine.
He did not know that their conversation had been a brief one which
ended with Tomsky screaming "Get out! Get the hell out of here!"
and using the foulest language, and then a shot, shortly after Stalin
had walked slowly away still holding his bottle of wine. Rykov had
also attempted suicide but his relatives had restrained him virtually

by force. Bukharin's first reaction was that Tomsky had finished them all off with his suicide, as if it were an admission of guilt on the part of the ex-"rightists." Later, when he met Rykov at a plenary session of the Central Committee, he said to him, "Tomsky was smarter than all of us."

We have already noted that on 21 August 1936, during the trial of Zinoviev and his comrades in misfortune, the public prosecutor, Vyshinsky, issued instructions for an inquiry into the affairs of Bukharin, Rykov, Tomsky, and other persons named in evidence as involved in a "counterrevolutionary plot." It is not easy to work out how this inquiry was conducted, since there were no interrogations or confrontations. Bukharin never went out and, naturally enough, never appeared in the offices of *Izvestiya*. Nevertheless the back page of the newspaper continued regularly to bear the legend, "Editor-in-chief: N. I. Bukharin." The "investigation" was soon completed and, although Bukharin was not questioned by anyone, on 10 September the central newspapers published a report from the public prosecutor's office to the effect that they had completed the investigation into "allegations made by some of the accused during the trial of those in the Trotskyite-Zinoviev Center concerning the greater or lesser degree of involvement of the criminal counterrevolutionary activities of N. I. Bukharin and A. I. Rykov." The report continued: "The investigation has produced no justification in law for the institution of legal proceedings against N. I. Bukharin and A. I. Rykov, on the strength of which the case in question is now regarded as closed."

Bukharin felt some relief at this, though naturally he noticed straightaway the ambiguity of the phrase "no justification in law." This lack of confidence in him was an insult to Bukharin. "It's like saying, 'He's got away with it,' " was what he told his friends and relations. Then again, the report mentioned only himself and Rykov. However, weary from all the stress, Bukharin left with his wife and little son (and a nanny) for one of the state-owned country dachas. He had no dacha of his own but as a candidate member of the Central Committee he did enjoy the right to relax at a state-owned one.

Karl Radek hurried out to see him late the following night. Radek was an extremely worried and frightened man. He gave Bukharin his assurance that he had nothing in common with any "counterrevolutionary" or "terrorist" activities of the "Trotskyite-Zinoviev Center." He asked Bukharin to write and tell Stalin everything when he (Radek) was arrested. "After all, the prosecutor's report only mentions Bukharin and Rykov, it doesn't say anything about the others. . . . Ask Stalin to deal with my case himself, not through Yagoda. . . . Remind Stalin about Blyumkin." Radek had in mind the Blyumkin affair. Blyumkin, a member of the party of leftist Social Revolutionaries and simultaneously a member of the recently formed Extraordinary Commission, had assassinated the German ambassador Mirbach early in June 1918. He was acting on instructions from his Central Committee which was counting on the concomitant provocation of Germany to declare war. Blyumkin was arrested and interrogated by Dzerzhinsky. The revolt of the leftist Social Revolutionaries had already been put down. Blyumkin not only gave Dzerzhinsky the whole story, he announced his own recantation and his break with the SRs. The circumstances of the times left little to choose between executing and sparing a man. Dzerzhinsky took to this decisive young man and he kept him in the Cheka. He was to serve for a short period as commander of Trotsky's train and he came under the latter's influence. Nevertheless he kept his job in the GPU in the 1920s and carried out a number of awkward assignments at home and abroad. During one journey to Turkey he visited Trotsky on the sly. Trotsky, naively trusting in the devotion of his followers, wrote a long letter and asked for it to be handed to Radek, which Blyumkin did once he got back to Moscow. Radek was scared stiff and took the letter, unopened, straight to Yagoda who passed it on to Stalin. Blyumkin was arrested without ceremony and soon shot. Radek had long since stopped making up jokes at Stalin's expense and now he considered that he had done enough to prove to the ever-suspicious Stalin that he was one hundred percent loyal. Now, standing in fear of arrest, he believed that Stalin would help him. A few days later Radek was indeed arrested. As soon as he learned of this Bukharin acted on his promise and wrote to Stalin outlining all that Radek had said. But the letter ended with the unworthy expression, "But who knows him anyway?"

Stalin spent nearly all of September at his dacha in Sochi. On 25 September he and Zhdanov sent a telegram to Kaganovich, Molotov, and the other Politburo members still in Moscow to the effect that Yagoda was to be sacked immediately from his post as people's commissar for home affairs and replaced by Yeshov, a comparatively young Party official who had suddenly come up in the world, having been elected to the Central Committee a mere two and a half years earlier and secretary of the Central Committee and chairman of Party Control only eighteen months ago. The removal of Yagoda and his replacement by Yeshov was not immediately taken to be a portent of increasing terror. Not many people were aware of the content of the telegram sent by Stalin and Zhdanov in which they justified the need to replace Yagoda on the grounds that OGPU had "fallen four years behind in the matter of exposing the Trotskyite-Zinoviev blok." Although there was comparatively little repression in the autumn of 1936 this seems to have been due to a series of political considerations, such as the discussion and adoption of the new constitution, and also to the fact that Yezhov had set about reconstructing the NKVD apparatus inherited from Yagoda. For some months before his appointment he had controlled the activities of the NKVD according to the Party line. On becoming people's commissar he replaced a number of people close to Yagoda and appointed to positions of responsibility several workers known for their loyalty to himself. All in all, however, it would be a mistake to exaggerate Yezhov's role. He was not a professional NKVD man and there were many refinements and specialities of that trade of which he remained ignorant. He lacked the requisite knowledge for work of such complexity as intelligence and counterintelligence, and was therefore incapable of entirely reconstructing the settled apparatus of the organization. He had to make many new appointments but in most cases he chose as his closest assistants professional security men such as Zakovsky, Redens, Frinovsky, etc. He not only carried out Stalin's instructions but did so blindly and slavishly. New trials and new repressions were prepared but these concepts originated not within the NKVD but in Stalin's head. As a first step many ex-Trotskyites, men such as Radek, were arrested that autumn, and the arrests were accompanied by a new and carefully prepared judicial scenario. The "success" of the recently completed Zinoviev-Kamenev trial encouraged Stalin to set up a new kind of "open" trial to which were invited not only specially selected representatives of the Soviet public but also correspondents of foreign newspapers and one or two other people representing Western countries.

Despite the announcement by the public prosecutor's office in September 1936 that the inquiry into the affairs of Bukharin and Rykov had been completed the arrival of a new head of the NKVD was marked by a renewal of that investigation. For Bukharin this meant difficult days ahead. According to a new practice introduced by Stalin the more important evidence and cross-examination of people under arrest was now being duplicated and circulated, marked "Secret," to all Central Committee members and candidates. Bukharin and Rykov were among those who received these dossiers from the NKVD. Bukharin had not the slightest idea of the methods by which the NKVD investigators forced their victims to incriminate both themselves and their comrades. He read all the evidence with horrified disbelief, understandably enough since the records of cross-examination included several mentions of his own name as that of one of the prominent organizers of terror and sabotage in the USSR. He could not imagine what he ought to do. His last hope was—Stalin. They had once been friends, or so it had seemed to Bukharin who still began all his letters to Stalin with the words "Dear Koba." They had spent a lot of time together, celebrated together, sung songs together (some of them not all that decent), and sometimes wrestled together—Bukharin, with his superior strength, used to throw Stalin and he would pick himself up from the grass with a joke and a rueful grin. At this time Bukharin wrote also to other earlier friends of his—Ordzhonikidze, Kalinin, Voroshilov. But Ordzhonikidze was going through a bad spell, his brother having been arrested as well as several of his friends. Kalinin did not answer his letters, but Voroshilov, who might also have simply kept quiet, suddenly sent over a brief, offensive note which read, "I beg you, Comrade Bukharin, never to approach me again with questions of any kind." This was written in a formal tone whereas previously the two of them had been on close terms, using the familiar second-person singular together.

Stalin did not reply to Bukharin, though he did try to keep Bukharin's hopes alive. According to Anna Larina, his wife, on 7 November 1936, the anniversary of the October Revolution, Bukharin decided to be in Red Square, though not as before on the stand above Lenin's tomb but on a side stand to which his pass as editor of *Izvestiya* gave him access. Stalin noticed him from his own stand and suddenly Anna saw a guard pressing his way through the dense crowd toward Bukharin. She expected that they would be asked to quit the square without further ado. But no, the guard saluted and said, "Comrade Bukharin, Comrade Stalin asks me to inform you that you are in the wrong place. Would you please proceed to the stand above the Tomb?"

However, immediately after the celebrations another bad spell began. Not in the Lubyanka but in the Kremlin Bukharin had to undergo a whole series of confrontations with arrested ex-Trotskyites and followers of his from the so-called Bukharin school. He faced among others, Sokolnikov, Serebriakov, and Radek. All of them described imaginary criminal contacts with Bukharin and the existence of yet another underground counterrevolutionary center headed by him. He denied everything but returned home from each examination in confusion and despair. One encounter, with Efim Tseitlin, who had been among his closest followers, particularly dismayed him; Tseitlin gave evidence in his presence that Bukharin had personally handed him a revolver and stationed him on a street-corner where Stalin was due to drive by but on that occasion Stalin had taken another route and the attempt had failed. All this evidence was being duplicated and circulated to Central Committee members. Bukharin returned home and took out his own revolver which had a gold plate attached to the handle with these words engraved on it: "To a leader of the Proletarian Revolution, N. I. Bukharin, from Klim Voroshilov." He now believed there was nothing left for him but to commit suicide. He said goodbye to his wife, shut himself up in his study, and sat there holding the revolver in his hand. But he could not bring himself to fire the shot. Later he was to go through this procedure several times. Sometimes in his wife's presence he would handle the revolver, gently toss it in the air, and then hide it away in his desk. These outbursts often ended in hysteria from which it took him a long time to recover. Despite all this he still found the strength to work and with the rise to power of Hitler this work now centered around anti-Fascist themes.

One afternoon, probably in late November 1936, a group of unknown people came to Bukharin's flat on Kremlin management business. This was a time when searches of the flats of people's commissars and Central Committee members were quite common and Bukharin assumed that it was his turn to have his flat searched. Worse than that, Bukharin was served notice of eviction from his Kremlin flat. Unprepared for anything like this, at first he panicked. He was especially concerned about his vast library and archives. How were they to be transported and where to? Suddenly the internal Kremlin telephone rang—it was Stalin. "Nikolai, how are things with you?" he inquired as if everything were perfectly normal. Bukharin answered in embarrassment that he was at that moment being served with an eviction order. Without more ado Stalin roared, "Tell them to get the hell out of there!" Needless to say, the uninvited guests left in haste.

In late November 1936 the Eighth Extraordinary Congress of Soviets was convened in Moscow to discuss and approve the new constitution of the USSR. Bukharin was still a member of the Central Executive Committee Union Council and the Constitution Commission; he also remained editor of *Izvestiya*, the organ of the Central Executive Committee and the All-Russian Central Executive Committee, and he was a candidate member of the Party Central Committee. Nevertheless he was almost certainly absent from the Extraordinary Congress of Soviets. In any case, when the congress elected an editorial commission with the task of finalizing the wording of the new constitution the name of Bukharin was conspicuously missing from it.

Ten

The Last Weeks of Freedom

———— »» «« ————

THE VARIOUS ORGANS of the NKVD, although immensely powerful, did not possess in 1936 the extraordinary authority which was invested in that organization at the plenary session of the Central Committee in June 1937. In the regions and republics local Party committees and also the Central Committee of the national Communist party still kept the activities of local NKVD units under fairly strict control. In order to arrest a member of the Party Central Committee or a member of the USSR Central Executive Committee it was necessary to have the approval not only of Stalin and one or two of his close comrades but of the whole Central Committee (or of the Central Executive Committee). The first member of the Central Committee to be elected at the Seventh Party Congress and arrested by the NKVD was Yu. L. Piatakov (normally referred to in documents of the 1920s as "G. L."). It is to be assumed that his arrest was sanctioned by one of the plenary sessions held in the late summer or early autumn of 1936. There is no means of knowing whether Nikolai Bukharin attended that meeting, the same one, apparently, which also approved the arrest of G. Sokolnikov, a candidate member. In December 1936 another plenary session turned its attention for the first time to the allegations leveled against Bukharin and Rykov. Every single speaker demanded the expulsion of the pair from the Central Committee and from the Party and thus the possibility of their being arrested. We need to bear in mind that they and all the other Central Committee members were receiving virtually every day secret copies of the "evidence" given by the "saboteurs" and "terrorists" already under arrest. The last person to speak was Stalin himself and he said abruptly that there was no need to hurry things—it was best to give the NKVD a chance to go more thoroughly into the question of the guilt or innocence of these two men. As a result the plenary session stopped short of sanctioning their arrest. Bukharin, as a candidate member of the Central Committee, continued to receive minutes taken down during the interrogation of various people under arrest. Personal confrontations also continued and with them further damning evidence against him.

Throughout December Bukharin maintained his policy of virtually never going out. He no longer took decisions for *Izvestiya* though he remained nominally the paper's editor-in-chief. Many people thought he had now been arrested. Then an important visitor arrived in the Soviet Union, the celebrated writer Lion Feuchtwanger, asking to meet Bukharin. Word was passed on through the Central Committee and Bukharin was asked to receive Feuchtwanger in the editorial office of *Izvestiya*. This was an attempt to demonstrate the "objectivity" of Soviet justice. Bukharin obeyed and drove to work to sit in his large editor's office for the last time. Even so Feuchtwanger never called. He seems to have had more important things to do that day, which may well mean that someone considered it inexpedient to arrange a meeting between him and Bukharin.

The new year, 1937, came in with a grand political trial, that of the so-called parallel center to which the NKVD "producers" assigned people who were for the most part ex-Trotskyites. They had in fact long since broken with Trotsky and, almost to a man, they had been restored to Party membership in the 1930s. They now occupied prominent positions in political bodies or institutions of state, or the press, etc. Piatakov, for instance, the chief accused, had served for several years as first deputy to the people's commissar for heavy industry. He was without doubt a more capable and more experienced administrator and economist (especially the latter) than Ordzhonikidze. Thus Piatakov was largely responsible for the creditable advances made in industrializing the Soviet Union during both the first two Five-Year Plans. Livshits had recently been promoted to deputy commissar for communications and both Sokolnikov and Serebriakov were prominent Party members.

This trial does not concern us here, though it is important to establish that during its course allegations were leveled against Bukharin so specifically that it became obvious that his days were numbered. The organizers of the trial deliberately selected as the men to make these allegations none other than Karl Radek, recently a worker on *Izvestiya*, who had visited Bukharin only a few months before at his cottage and asked him to intercede on his (Radek's) behalf. Once Radek was arrested he did not keep his mouth shut for long waiting for intimidation and torture. He began quickly cooperating with the inquiry and helping the investigators to create the legend of a "parallel center" and its contacts with "exposed" and "unexposed" "counterforced revolutionary" organizations. It was probably due to Radek's forced assistance that the 1937 trial was prepared so quickly and went so smoothly. It is well known that Radek was not sentenced to be shot but given a ten-year prison sentence. The indications are that he also helped prepare the similar "legend" used in the 1938 trial and that during the confrontations with men under arrest he persuaded them to sign all the falsified evidence drummed up by the investigators. It was he who made the most serious allegations against Bukharin, particularly this concluding statement made on 29 January 1937:

I admit to one further fault. Having confessed all my faults and exposed the organization, I stubbornly refused to give evidence against Bukharin. I knew that Bukharin's position was as hopeless as mine since our guilt, if not actually ascertainable in law, was as good as that in essence. But we were close friends and intellectual friendship is stronger than any other. I knew that Bukharin was in the same state of shock as I was and I did not doubt that he would give honest evidence to the Soviet authorities. I did not therefore wish to deliver him bound hand and foot to the Ministry of the Interior. As with the remainder of our personnel I also wanted him to have the chance to lay down his arms. This explains why only at the last moment when the court was there in front of my nose did I realize that I could not appear before the court while still concealing the existence of another terrorist organization.[1]

In mid-January Bukharin and Rykov were officially dismissed from their posts. The 17 January edition of *Izvestiya* appeared with no indication that Bukharin was the editor-in-chief. Many people jumped to the conclusion that he had been arrested, but this was not the case. He lived on in his Kremlin flat under voluntary house arrest, still receiving his Kremlin rations as a candidate member of the Central Committee (naturally he kept away from the Kremlin dining room) and still writing letters to Stalin beginning as always in the past, "Dear Koba. . . ."

Shortly after the end of the Radek-Piatakov trial a plenary session of the Central Committee was announced. Members were informed that it would take place on 19 February. There were two main items on the agenda: (1.) N. Bukharin and A. Rykov and (2.) preparing Party organizations for the elections to the Supreme Soviet.

When he received the notice Bukharin realized that it could only be a question of his and Rykov's expulsion from the Central Committee and the Party. Accordingly, unable to discover any other way of fighting back, Bukharin decided to go on a hunger strike. He refused to accept any food and informed Stalin of his decision, probably along with one or two other Central Committee members.

Sergo Ordzhonikidze committed suicide on 18 February 1937. His flat adjoined Bukharin's though the entries were different. Bukharin was very fond of Ordzhonikidze, whom he trusted. Learning of his death from radio and press reports, he believed the official version of his death as the result of a heart attack. He could not visit Sergo's flat or attend his funeral, however. A few days after the start of his hunger strike Bukharin rang Stalin. "Who are you striking against? The Party?" Stalin wanted to know. "What can I do if you're getting ready to expel me from the Party?" "No one's getting ready to expel you from the Party," said Stalin and hung up.

Ordzhonikidze's funeral caused them to delay the plenary session for a week. A couple of days in advance Central Committee members received a new agenda with the following items: (1.) N. Bukharin and A. Rykov, (2.) Bukharin's hunger strike—action against the Party, and (3.) preparation of Party organizations for the elections to the Supreme Soviet.

Bukharin was in a quandary when he received these papers. If the agenda included his hunger strike as its second item, he reasoned both to himself and aloud to his wife, that meant that Rykov and he were not about to be expelled. No one would want to launch into a discussion of a hunger strike declared by an ex-member of the Central Committee who had just been expelled. Bukharin ended his hunger strike.

The meeting opened on 25 February. Yezhov made an announcement concerning Bukharin and Rykov and their "activities as spies and saboteurs." Then the members began to make their speeches. There exists a legend that one or two of them defended the two accused and spoke out against the mass repression which had begun. It is not so. To a man they condemned Bukharin and Rykov and demanded that proceedings be taken against them. The speeches included innumerable instances of sabotage carried out by the ex-members of the opposition in various areas of the economy and the culture. Postyshev's speech was the only one to express any doubts about the propriety of arresting a close colleague who had never indulged in oppositional activity. But Postyshev himself was vulnerable at that time. Only in January he had been relieved of his duties as first secretary of the Kiev Regional Party Committee though he kept his position as second secretary to the Kiev Party Central Committee. The Kiev plenary session was chaired by Lazar Kaganovich who used a slanderous letter from one Nikolayevko to destroy the regional committee. Its leaders stood accused of a whole series of political errors, red tape, and contacts with "Trotskyites." One man who spoke out very strongly against Bukharin and Rykov was V. M. Molotov.

The atmosphere was truly heated when Bukharin's turn came to speak. He denied all the charges and said, "I am no Zinoviev or Kamenev. I'm not going to tell lies against myself." Molotov shouted from his seat, "No confession! That proves you're a Fascist hireling—their press is always writing that our trials are provocative—arrest and confession!" "It's a trap!" exclaimed Bukharin when he got home. He wanted to defend himself against slander but didn't want to "assist the Fascists." Bukharin read out to the plenary session a joint declaration made by himself and Rykov to the effect that the evidence brought against them during the Piatakov-Radek trial and by other individuals under arrest was all slanderous. They accused the NKVD of fabricating false evidence and proposed the setting up of a commission to review the activities of that organization. Stalin called out "We'll send you down there—you can see for yourself."

In order to settle the case of these two men the plenary session set up a commission about thirty-strong and meanwhile called a two-day halt in proceedings. Bukharin spent the time at home. He was now without hope. He wrote a letter "To the future generation of Party leaders" which he asked his wife to learn by heart. "You're still young. You'll live to see other people at the head of the Party." He tested her throughout the two days until he was satisfied that she was word perfect. This was how the letter began.

I am leaving this life. I bow my head not before the ax of the proletariat, which is necessarily merciless but nevertheless pure. I feel my own impotence before a devilish machine which, by using in all probability medieval methods, has come to possess a gigantic power, enough to fabricate organized slander, and to act with forthright boldness. . . .

Bukharin went on to make a series of accusations against the NKVD which had turned into an organization of degenerate, corrupt, empty-headed and fat-bellied civil servants carrying out their vile practices in order to please the "sick, suspicious mind of Stalin—I daren't say more than that." He rejected all the allegations against himself, Rykov, and Tomsky, but did not refer to those concerning the other condemned ex-members of the opposition. Emphasizing his own loyalty he wrote that he had not had "the slightest vestige of disagreement with the Party for nearly seven years."

I turn to you, the future generation of Party leaders whose historical mission includes an obligation to disentangle the ghastly tissue of crimes which in these terrible days is spreading on a grand scale, burning up like a flame and choking the Party. I turn to all Party members! In these, probably the last days of my life, I am certain that sooner or later the filter of history will inevitably wash the filth from my head. I have never been a traitor, I would have given my life unhesitatingly to save Lenin's, I loved Kirov and I have never plotted against Stalin. I ask the new, young, and honest generation of Party leaders to have my letter read out at a plenary session to vindicate my name and restore me in the eyes of the Party.

Bukharin made a final check of his wife's memory and then burned the letter.

The commission entrusted with resolving the Bukharin-Rykov issue sat under A. I. Mikoyan. It included almost all the high-level Party leaders, many of whom were themselves to perish over the next couple of years, victims of cruel repression. When it came to take a decision a vote was taken, name by name, in alphabetical order. One after another members of the Central Committee rose to their feet, Andreyev, Bubnov, Voroshilov . . . and they all said the same: "To be arrested, brought to trial, and shot." When Stalin's turn came he said, "Transfer this matter to the NKVD." One or two others repeated this formula but the majority wanted the two "to be arrested, brought to trial, and shot." (Mikoyan alone, as chairman, stated no opinion and none is recorded in the minutes.)

After the two-day delay the plenary session was reconvened. Bukharin and Rykov were summoned before it in order to hear the decision that had been reached. Bukharin had no doubts that his fate was sealed. He kissed his nine-month-old son, fell weeping at his wife's feet, and begged her forgiveness. He realized she was in for a hard time but he had no conception of everything which he and she would yet have to endure. He got a grip on himself and said, "Anya, don't forget—I'm not guilty of anything. History has its ups and downs. Bring up our son to be a strong Bolshevik."

The session was being held in the Kremlin where the Bukharins lived. All he had to do was cross the yard and enter the building where the meeting was under way. The cloakroom was deserted. Rykov came in at exactly the same time as Bukharin. As they were handing in their overcoats eight men walked forward from the wall and approached Bukharin and Rykov, four apiece. This was the arrest. They were taken from the Central Committee building straight to the Lubyanka. Simultaneously NKVD officials arrived in Bukh-

arin's flat to start a search. Bukharin's wife realized she would
never see her husband again. The search went on and on. The library was left largely untouched but all Bukharin's papers and archives were confiscated and taken away. The archives contained
many priceless documents including a large number of letters from
Lenin. Soon after Lenin's death the Party Central Committee
requested all Party members to hand in to the Lenin Institute,
which was being set up at the time, any remaining letters, notes,
and other documents written by Lenin or pertaining to his activities. Bukharin had then presented a good number of Lenin documents to the directorate of the new institute, but he had kept back a
lot of letters and notes which were of a personal nature.

Although the search was taking a long time it was at least being
conducted with comparative courtesy. No members of Bukharin's
family were arrested. At the time the flat was occupied not only by
his wife, his son, and the nanny, but also by his father who had once
been a primary-school teacher. He was well over seventy and
seriously ill. After the arrest of Bukharin, his father, who was so
proud of his son, lived on for a few years. He died shortly before the
war, having outlived his son by a short period.

Back in 1936 when the newspapers announced that the inquiry
into Bukharin's and Rykov's contacts with the Zinoviev "terrorist
group" had completed its work Bukharin received a greetings telegram from Romain Rolland and a letter from Boris Pasternak. Once
it became known in Moscow that Bukharin had been arrested Pasternak immediately wrote a letter and had it taken to Anna Larina.
In it he stated that he had not the slightest doubt of Nikolai's innocence. This time Romain Rolland did not react to events in
Moscow.

Eleven

The Investigation

PRACTICALLY NOTHING RELIABLE is known about the way in which the "investigation" of Bukharin's case was carried out, though it lasted rather more than a year. We do have scattered bits of testimony about the manner of the investigation from some of the people who survived many years of horror in Stalin's labor camps and prisons. Some of this material appears highly credible whereas other parts of it are obviously unreliable. For instance, Iosif Berger's book tells of a meeting with Aleksandr Aykhenvald, a follower of Bukharin, in one of the camps.

Aleksandr was one of those who was made to confront Bukharin personally shortly before the trial began. The confrontation lasted almost five hours. The investigator asked Aleksandr about various episodes in Bukharin's life in the early thirties when Bukharin was still a member of the Central Committee. Aleksandr was forced to repeat evidence of conversations he had had with Bukharin. What had emerged from them, although Bukharin did not state this directly, was that in the peasant uprisings and economic chaos he saw proof of the collapse of Stalin's policy of collectivized agriculture. Bukharin did not deny the general tone of these conversations but he tried to prevent the inquiry from drawing dangerous conclusions from them. He was very annoyed that Aleksandr said so much. Aleksandr justified his conduct by saying that he wasn't being a "Pinkerton"—he firmly denied the existence of any plot and the slightest involvement of Bukharin in terrorist activity. He claimed that Bukharin was exclusively a man of ideas and no criminal. After certain small differences over detailed wording Bukharin usually consented to sign the record. . . . At the end of the confrontation Bukharin was totally reconciled with Aykhenvald and he asked the investigator if they could speak together for a few minutes alone. This was allowed and the investigator left the office, leaving only a guard at the door. Bukharin and Aykhenvald spent two hours together, facing each other and without witnesses. First and foremost Bukharin wanted to know about his own family and the fate of his followers. Then he told Aykhenvald his philosophical views as they related to the past. He was being allowed to read and write in prison. Books were brought for him and he was allowed a typewriter. He was writing a book. When Aleksandr asked what it was about he received an answer which surprised him, "About the nature of man." Bukharin went so far as to attempt to convince Aykhenvald that from now on he was to concentrate on one thing alone: to forget questions of ideology, economics, and politics and to attempt to understand the meaning and value of life in general. From what Aykhenvald told me I was not able exactly to pinpoint what conclusions Bukharin had come to or even whether his searchings were mystical, purely ethical, or philosophical in nature. But this is what Bukharin was working on during the last days of his life.[1]

We have no cause for doubting that Aykhenvald was brought into personal confrontation with Bukharin, perhaps more than once, though it does seem doubtful that the investigator was kind enough to allow Bukharin and his follower two hours of private conversation. Bukharin was being prepared for an open trial, which placed a special responsibility on the investigator. Total isolation from the outside world was only one of the vital conditions involved. It is true that Bukharin was allowed to read and write in his prison cell, but we shall see below that, at least during the earlier months of his imprisonment, he was writing a quite different book. It is improbable in the extreme that Bukharin could have advised his follower to forget about politics and economics. He could not have asked Aykhenvald about his family since Aykhenvald was himself arrested earlier than Bukharin.

Maria Ioffe, the widow of the well-known Party worker A. A. Ioffe, has written a book called *One Long Night* and subtitled "A story of the truth." What her book has to say about Bukharin, however, is very far from the truth. Here is an extract.

Vasilchin got up very slowly off his dry log and stood silent for a while. . . . Then he spoke, slowly, as if unwillingly:

'By a bonfire in a wood I once gave a promise to someone who had been a witness to and gave me the most extraordinary information regarding the last hours of Nikolai Ivanovich Bukharin. This promise was never to reveal this information to anyone. But now this no longer holds. I've heard that someone has already made it public, either verbally or in print. And anyway, I doubt if my informant is still alive.

'Next to the place where "action was taken" was the hall of the "Troika" meetings. Bukharin was taken in there and seated at a table. The soldiers who led him in carried revolvers. Following them, there came in a thoroughly confused, ordinary working-class woman, carrying a string bag full of shopping and accompanied by a little girl clinging to her skirts. The woman was babbling, almost incoherently: "I . . . I just don't understand anything . . . I came out of the shop and the driver of a car, a rather shabby car, beckoned to me and said, there now, we are going the same way—get in and I'll give you a lift—just look what a load you've collected, and then he brought me here. . . ."

'At that moment, a chief of four-star rank came in and said: "Nikolai Ivanovich, let me tell you that if you do not write, in your own handwriting on this sheet of paper, a signed confession that even prior to the Revolution you carried out tasks for foreign intelligence—this woman and her child will be shot right here. Please bear in mind that this order comes from above and as such cannot be discussed." Bukharin jumped up: "What? Announce to the whole world, to all the workers, that the proletarian revolution in Russia was carried out by traitors, betrayers and spies?—Never!"

' "But you will then be the murderer of these innocent people." The revolvers were pointed at the woman and her child. "When I wave my hand—fire . . ." said the chief to his soldiers and again turned to Bukharin. "Well?"—"Never," the reply came firmly and quietly.

'The chief gave a wave of the hand . . . the corpses were still in the hall when Nikolai Ivanovich Bukharin was finished off in the next room.'

Everyone took off their hats.

'I am certain that the person who told me was one of those who carried out this deed. It was not possible for anyone else to have been there . . .' concluded the Professor.[2]

There can be no doubt that this is one of those labor camp *parashas,* that is, rumors often made up in the camp themselves. Such an episode could not have occurred before Bukharin's trial and after the trial and sentencing it would have been without any meaning. It has been established from many sources that as early as 1930–31 the GPU did use in the course of its inquiries a method by which a man under investigation might be brought to watch an execution and sometimes he would be told that if he agreed to sign a certain document the next man to be executed would be spared. This often had the desired effect. However, there were no executions of children or innocent passers-by in the street. After a "session" of this kind the man under investigation would be taken back to his cell "to think things over." It is by no means out of the question that during his own investigation Bukharin was taken to observe the execution of other prisoners, perhaps people he knew, his own followers. As the rumors about this sort of thing passed from mouth to mouth, however, they appear to have sprouted all manner of spurious details.

When discussing the "investigation" of Bukharin's case and considering the various hypotheses concerning his behaviour while it was under way we can scarcely ignore Arthur Koestler's novel *Darkness At Noon*. Koestler emigrated from Hungary in the 1920s and, after many wanderings, settled in England. He wrote *Darkness At Noon* in 1940 and it rapidly became world-famous. The hero of the novel, Nikolay Salmanowitch Rubashov is a Soviet people's commissar, one of the foremost leaders of the Communist party and Comintern. He is arrested and two investigators, Ivanov and Gletkin, are given the job of "preparing" him for a public trial. Rubashov is not tortured like the naval commander Bagrov. He is not mocked like many other prisoners. He is required to perform "one last service" for the Party, to invoke hatred in the people for any form of opposition and thus to guarantee that they will rally round the leadership of the Party in the period preceding inevitable war. Rubashov himself had once belonged to the opposition and fought against the "No. 1" who became the unchallenged dictator of the country and who was steadily eliminating the "old guard." However, he had come round to acknowledge No. 1 as being in the right and begun to carry out his orders conscientiously, which did not prevent him from landing up in prison. After a long series of interrogations Rubashov agrees to confess to part of the evidence against him. He says to the investigator:

'I plead guilty to not having understood the fatal compulsion behind the policy of the Government, and to have therefore held oppositional views. . . . I have lent my ear to the lament of the sacrificed, and thus became deaf to the arguments which proved the necessity to sacrifice them. . . . I know that my aberration, if carried into effect, would have been a mortal danger to the Revolution. Every opposition at the critical turning-points of history, carries in itself the germ of a split in the Party, and hence the germ of civil war. Humanitarian weakness and liberal democracy, when the masses are not mature, is suicide for the revolution. And yet my oppositional attitude was based on a craving for just these methods—in appearance so desirable, actually so deadly. On a demand for a liberal reform of the dictatorship; for a broader democracy, for the abolition of the Terror, and a loosening of the rigid organization of the Party. I admit that these demands, in the present situation, are objectively harmful and therefore counter-revolution in character. . . .'

He paused again. . . .[3]

But the inquiry does not consider these admissions to be sufficient. The investigator reads out an extract from Rubashov's own diary:

It is necessary to hammer every sentence into the masses by repetition and simplification. What is presented as right must shine like gold; what is presented as wrong must be black as pitch.[4]

It was required of Rubashov not only that he acknowledge his ideas to have been pernicious and counterrevolutionary. He had also to admit in open court that he had engaged in wrecking and sabotage, had encouraged Terror and planned the murder of the Leader. Finally he was called upon to confess that he had been the paid agent of a foreign power.

Rubashov was silent. Then he said:
'So, that is what you are aiming at: I am to play the Devil in your Punch and Judy show—howl, grind my teeth and put out my tongue—and voluntarily, too. Danton and his friends were spared that, at least.'

Gletkin shut the cover of the dossier. He bent forward a bit and settled his cuffs:
'Your testimony at the trial will be the last service you can do the Party. . . . The Party must be as if cast from one mould—filled with blind discipline and absolute trust. You and your friends, Citizen Rubashov, have made a rent in the Party. If your repentance is real, then you must help us to heal this rent. I have told you, it is the last service the Party will ask of you.'[5]

And gradually Rubashov gives in. Each time, after a tenacious argument with his investigator, he puts his name to a new admission. At last he signs the complete confession. Gletkin is now satisfied. He even goes so far as to address the accused as "Comrade Rubashov." But he goes on to say

'Observe . . . that the Party holds out to you no prospect of reward. Some of the accused have been made amenable by physical pressure. Others, by the promise to save their heads—or the heads of their relatives who had fallen into our hands as hostages. To you, Comrade Rubashov, we propose no bargain and we promise nothing. . . . You were wrong, and you will pay Comrade Rubashov. The Party promises only one thing: after the victory, one day when it can do no more harm, the material of the secret archives will be published. Then the world will learn what was in the background of this Punch and Judy show—as you called it—which we had to act to them according to history's text-book. . . . And then you, and some of your friends of the older generation, will be given the sympathy and pity which are denied to you today.'[6]

Arthur Koestler did not deny that in creating the character of Rubashov he drew on some of the features of Piatakov and Radek but his chief model was Nikolai Bukharin—as he himself understood and imagined Bukharin, of course. The novel contains many inaccuracies and mistakes, which is hardly surprising since at the time it was written there had been no rehabilitation and nothing like the subsequent flow of memoirs and research work concerning Stalinist repression. In the first pages of the novel we read that in the prison to which Rubashov was taken in every cell a little placard was mounted bearing the name of the inmate. Stalin's prisons, of course, contained nothing of the kind. But the methods of investigation certainly included attempts to persuade men under arrest to perform a "last service for the Party" through their slanderous self-accusation. There were also people who consented to play the role of the Devil in a "Punch and Judy show." However, Bukharin is not likely to have been one of these. Well before his arrest he declared to the Party plenary session that he would never slander himself as Zinoviev and Kamenev had done. It is conceivable that Bukharin was never tortured, though one cannot depend on it. Without a doubt he was threatened that if he failed to cooperate with the inquiry his young wife and baby son would be eliminated. This is quite clear from the attitude taken by the authorities to Bukharin's family after his arrest.

For almost a week after the arrest Anna stayed at home in her flat. But the baby had to be taken out into the fresh air and soon she began to take him for a stroll around the Kremlin in his baby carriage. No one approached her; no one asked her anything. After a while, however, someone telephoned to ask why she was not collecting her rations. "What rations?" "You qualify for rations." These, of course, related to Nikolai's high position. She thought there was some misunderstanding and did not fetch her rations. However, the nanny was sent for and she brought food back with her. They did not refuse it. Bukharin had neither savings nor stores and after his arrest the family was soon without money or supplies.

It was probably about a month after the arrest that an NKVD official arrived with a note from Nikolai asking his wife to send over a few books and other materials. He wrote that he had begun work on a book to be entitled "The Degradation of Culture Under Fascism," and these things were necessary for his work. She was not in a position to release anything, however, since his library had been sealed off. Soon afterwards a telephone call came from the chief investigator and she was given permission to break the seals on the study door in order to go in and get the books requested. She was asked to bring them herself to the Lubyanka. She did so, and took along some food as well but this was refused. The investigator told her, "Your husband is being well fed. . . . Yes, and he's got a sweet tooth, hasn't he? We're giving him six lumps of sugar with every glass of tea." He went on to say, "Your husband has asked you to write him a note and send a photograph of yourself and your son." Anna began to write her note but the investigator interrupted her to dictate what she could, indeed what she must, write. "Write that you are living as before in your old flat in the Kremlin and receiving rations." "I won't write that," she replied, sensing that some kind of dirty trick was being played. If that was what they wanted, that was what they were not going to get. After their altercation the investigator refused to accept Anna's note without the words he had dictated.

Despite Bukharin's arrest, and the mass arrests now occurring

throughout the country and even beginning to affect members of
the Party Central Committee, Bukharin's family continued to live
on in the Kremlin. Life there, however, soon became intolerable.
No one would have anything to do with the family of such a prominent "enemy of the people." Anna Larina asked for an exchange and
some days later she was offered a five-room flat in the "house on the
embankment," the block of government flats near to the Kremlin
but on the embankment across the river Moscow. This was a period
when flats there were becoming available all the time; in fact the
block was half empty. At the end of the month Anna received a bill
in respect of rent and services. She owed three hundred rubles
which even at the time was a substantial sum of money. Previous oc-
cupants of those flats would have found it insignificant but not Anna
Larina. She sent the bill to Kalinin with a terse note: "Unfortunately
the Gestapo spy Bukharin was paid too little for his services and we
do not have the kind of money needed to pay for this flat." When
Kalinin got the note he made arrangements for Bukharin's family to
live on there free of charge. Not that they lived there for long. In
the summer of 1937 Anna Larina was arrested and soon afterwards
exiled to Astrakhan where she spent about a year. We must assume
that Bukharin had now begun to give the required evidence to the
inquiry and there was no reason to pussy-foot with his family.

During the investigation into his case, in May 1937, Bukharin
was expelled from the Academy of Sciences. A general meeting of
the Academy passed the following resolution:

In view of the fact that Bukharin has used his position in the Academy to
harm our country and, through his opposition to the Party and the Soviet
government, has placed himself in the ranks of the enemies of our people,
under Regulation No. 24 of the USSR Academy of Sciences it is resolved to
expel N. I. Bukharin from the presidium of the academy and to bring this
resolution to the attention of the Council of People's Commissars.[7]

Twelve

The Trial

>> <<

THE TRIAL in the case of the "Anti-Soviet Rightist-Trotskyite Bloc" opened on 2 March 1938. In many respects it was the most important of all the trials, a kind of summation of all the preceding ones purporting to expose the most secret and the widest ranging, in terms of the numbers involved, of all the anti-Soviet centers. Bukharin was the chief defendant. With him in the dock were A. I. Rykov, for many years head of the Council of People's Commissars, other people's commissars such as A. P. Rozengolts, M. A. Chernov, G. F. Grinko, V. I. Ivanov, and also the ex-head of the NKVD, later people's commissar for communications, G. G. Yagoda. Among the others accused were the prominent diplomat and one of the oldest Party workers, N. N. Krestinsky; the celebrated activist in the Russian and international workers' movement, Kh. G. Rakovsky; the leaders of the Uzbek Republic, A. Ikramov and F. Khodzhayev; Maxim Gorky's secretary, P. P. Kryuchkov; and several doctors.

A large body of literature has grown up around the so-called open political trials of the period 1936–38 and many of the aspects of these show-trials are outside the scope of the present analysis. This is not the occasion to attempt a thoroughgoing consideration of all the available information on this subject and the various hypotheses, versions, and proposals relating to it.

Alexander Solzhenitsyn devotes a few pages of his *Gulag Archipelago* to these trials and it must be said that the facts evinced by him, especially with regard to Bukharin, do correspond to reality. The reader of the *Gulag* will not fail to notice, however, the strangely malicious pleasure with which Solzehenitsyn writes about the accused, particularly Bukharin. The author cannot hide his satisfaction at the punishment meted out by Stalin to his former opponents and he clearly accords Stalin greater respect than his victims. Here is a typical passage:

> Dumbfounded, the world watched three plays in a row, three wide-ranging and expensive dramatic productions in which the powerful leaders of the fearful Communist Party who had turned the entire world upside-down and terrified it now marched forth like doleful, obedient goats and bleated out everything they had been ordered to, vomited all over themselves, cringingly abased themselves and their convictions, and confessed to crimes they could not in any wise have committed. This was unprecedented in remembered history. It was particularly astonishing in contrast with the recent Leipzig trial of Dimitrov. Dimitrov had answered the Nazi judges like a roaring lion and immediately afterwards his comrades in Moscow, members of the same unyielding cohort which had made the whole world tremble—and the greatest of them at that, those who had been called the 'Leninist guard'—came before the judges drenched in their own urine.[1]

As Solzhenitsyn sees it the only tragedy was the punishment of their political opponents by the Bolsheviks during the first years of revolution. The trials and repressions of 1936–38 were a comedy rather than a tragedy and a further excuse to pour scorn on the hated Bolsheviks. Such clearly ignoble conduct in the depiction of a new stream of *Gulag* internees and victims of Stalin creates a particularly revolting impression when Solzhenitsyn proclaims himself a Christian and asserts that Christianity is the one doctrine capable of renewing Russia and creating new relationships between people. It is strange that in the very same volume of *The Gulag Archipelago* Solzhenitsyn describes his own cowardly conduct when under investigation. On this occasion the events are outlined with a quite different intonation.

> Looking back on my interrogation from my long subsequent imprisonment I had no reason to be proud of it. I might have borne myself more firmly and in all probability could have maneuvered more skilfully. But my first weeks were characterised by a mental blackout and a slump into depression. The only reason these recollections do not torment me with re-

morse is that, thanks to God, I avoided getting anyone else arrested. But I came close to it.[2]

Following his interrogation sessions in which no one tortured him or even "put him on the conveyor belt,"* Solzhenitsyn was handed a file dealing with his "case." He himself gives us the following testimony.

I turned more pages. I saw photocopies of my own letters and a totally distorted interpretation of their meaning by unknown commentators. . . . I saw the hyperbolized lies in which Captain Yezepov had wrapped up my careful testimony. And, last but not least, I saw the idiocy whereby I, one individual, was accused as a 'group'!

'I won't sign.' I said without much firmness. 'You conducted the interrogation improperly!'

'Alright then, let's begin all over again!' Maliciously he compressed his lips. 'We'll send you off to a place where we keep the Polizei. . . .'

Somewhere outside the fifth-floor windows of the Lubyanka the golden sunset glowed. Somewhere it was May. . . . Begin all over again? It seemed to me it would be easier to die than to begin all over again. Ahead of me loomed at least some kind of life. . . . And then what about the place where they kept the Polizei? And, in general, it was a bad idea to make him angry. It would influence the tone in which he phrased the conclusion of the indictment.

And so I signed. I signed it complete with Section 11 ['organisation']. . . . But because of that Section 11 I was later put into a hard-labour camp. Because of that Section 11 I was sent, even after 'liberation' and without any additional sentence into eternal exile. Maybe it was all for the best. Without both these experiences I would not have written this book. . . .[3]

Such is Solzhenitsyn's description of himself, though he pours scorn upon Bukharin who had to undergo incomparably more arduous moral and physical suffering. However, it is not part of our purpose in this book to arrive at moral evaluations, or to condemn any of those who stood accused. Let us limit ourselves to the main facts.

The judicial session of the Military Collegium of the Supreme Court of the USSR took place in the October Hall of the House of Soviets (and not, as many people think, in the Column Room). There was room for about five hundred people. The first five rows

---

*Translator's note: The phrase "conveyor belt" refers to a method of continuous interrogation mounted by a team of officials working in shifts with the aim of wearing down a prisoner by depriving him of rest.

were occupied by members of the NKVD. Behind them sat representatives of the general public, most of whom knew each other
though they included people unknown to anyone else. These latter
were probably also NKVD men. I do not put inverted commas
around the representatives of the general public since they were actually people who represented the various circles of Soviet society
and the Soviet press. Many of them were issued with passes valid
for only one day. Among them were, to give a couple of examples,
the famous Soviet artist Moskvin and Ilya Ehrenburg who was informed that Stalin had personally ensured that he was not to be
short of a pass. "Make sure Ehrenburg gets a pass," Stalin is said to
have ordered the new editor of *Izvestiya*. "Let him watch his little
friend."

At the start of the trial the members of the Judicial Collegium
came out and took their places—the president, V. V. Ulrikh, jurists
I. O. Matulevich and B. I. Ievlev, and the secretary, A. A. Batner.
Then in came the state prosecutor, Andrei Ya. Vyshinsky and coun-
sels for the defence, I. D. Braude and N. V. Kommodov. They were
followed on to the scene by the first group of guards. In front of each
accused sat his own investigator, that is, the particular NKVD official who was dealing with his case and had "prepared" the accused
for the final show. The hall contained boxes accommodating representatives of the foreign press and next door was a room where
foreign correspondents could type out their reports and comments.
Among the English correspondents, for example, were G. MacLean
and Edmund Stevens, the latter a young man representing the
Manchester Guardian, though now he lives in Moscow in a large
well-appointed house on Ryleyev Street as representative of the
Sunday Times, one of the most dependable of the English papers.
The chief foreign guest at the Bukharin-Rykov trial, as at that of
Radek and Piatakov, was the special ambassador of the US president, Joseph E. Davies. He was not a Russian-speaker and his interpreting was carried out by the English correspondent of an
American newspaper—Shapiro. Despite this the two of them were
to arrive at different conclusions. Shapiro considered the trial to be
a falsified piece of play-acting whereas Davies arrived at the belief
that Stalin had crushed a fifth column in the Soviet Union, an idea

which he expressed in letters to his daughter during the trial, in his report to President Roosevelt, and in his book *Mission to Moscow* published in 1941.[4]

Next came the accused who were placed sitting behind a barrier in the dock. They differed in appearance. Khodzhayev was dressed in a splendid suit which looked as if it had just been made. Ikramov, on the other hand, was untidily turned out; he seemed like a broken man who had gone to pieces. Yagoda had the air of a large wolf now beaten into submission. Krestinsky (in the words of correspondent MacLean) was "a pale, wan, seedy figure with steel-rimmed spectacles on his hawk nose." Bukharin was pale-faced and wore a look of intense concentration.

Once a number of procedural questions had been disposed of the secretary of the court read out the extensive indictment based upon materials obtained during the preliminary inquiry. Then the president, Ulrikh, addressed the same question to each of the accused in turn: "Do you plead guilty to the charges brought against you?" Bukharin, Rykov, and Yagoda all said, "Yes, I do." But when Krestinsky's turn came he suddenly replied in a loud, harsh, faltering voice, "I plead not guilty. I am not a Trotskyite. I have never been a member of the Rightist and Trotskyite Bloc, of whose existence I was not aware. Nor have I committed any of the crimes with which I personally am charged; in particular I plead not guilty to the charge of having had connections with the German intelligence service." Ulrikh, somewhat taken aback, repeated his question and received the same firm reply. Upon which Ulrikh proceeded to the other accused all of whom pleaded guilty. Then a twenty-minute adjournment was announced.

From the events that followed it is possible to conclude that during the adjournment a decision was taken to change the order for cross-examining the accused. It was decided to begin with the cross-examination of Bessonov whose planned role in the organization of the trial scenario was a crucial one. He had been given the part of that person who, ostensibly, linked the Trotskyites and Zinovievites with the "rightists," which meant Bukharin, Rykov, and Tomsky in particular. He was the one who, working as he did as a Soviet trade representative in Berlin, had seemingly organized occasions for the oppositionists to meet Trotsky and his son, Sedov, and handed over directives and other such materials. It is difficult to blame Bessonov who took some persuading to accept this role at the trial. During the preliminary investigation he was subjected to every last refinement in physical torture and he showed stubborn resistance. At the very start of the investigation he was held on the "conveyor belt" for seventeen days and nights without sleep or food. He fell down and lost consciousness but they brought him round, lifted him back, and, as investigator followed investigator shift by shift, they kept on asking him always the same questions. Then they began to beat him, methodically, until this strong, healthy man was reduced to an invalid. But, as in so many similar cases, Bessonov was eventually broken and compelled to sign the first false documents. He simply had no strength left in him to resist further and thus became an obedient weapon in the hands of the trial organizers.

Thus it was that the morning session on 2 March began with the cross-examination of Bessonov. The interrogation of each accused was usually accompanied by occasional questions addressed to other defendants for purposes of confirmation. When Bessonov spoke of his efforts to link the Trotskyites and Zinovievites with the "rightists" Vyshinsky turned to Bukharin—could he confirm Bessonov's evidence? Bukharin replied that talks with Piatakov and other Trotskyites had been conducted by the "rightists" even before Bessonov's time. "You were carrying on negotiations . . . concerning united operations against Soviet power?" "Yes," was Bukharin's answer. However, when Vyshinsky turned to Krestinsky for confirmation of further evidence given by Bessonov, Krestinsky denied everything. A prominent Party worker and political figure, Krestinsky had, until his arrest, held the post of deputy commissar for foreign affairs. He had not been a Trotskyite and had taken no part in the Party infighting of the 1920s mainly because of nine years (1921–30) he had served as Soviet ambassador in Germany. During the investigation he had been quick to agree to the investigator's version of events and had signed whatever statements had been demanded of him. As things turned out he had realized that a new political trial was being prepared and he had decided to conserve his strength and tell the truth at the trial itself.

In a harsh voice, penetratingly loud, Krestinsky declared that never, in any place and at any time, had he spoken with Bessonov about Trotskyites, he had never been a Trotskyite and that Bessonov was lying to the court. When the dismayed Vyshinsky asked him about his deposition made during the preliminary investigation, Krestinsky replied that it was false. "Why did you not tell the truth during the preliminary investigation?" asked Vyshinsky. Krestinsky hesitated before replying and Vyshinsky hastened to finish his interrogation with the words, "I hear no reply. No further questions." He then proceeded to reinterrogate Bessonov apparently in order to give a chance for the investigator sitting beside Krestinsky to warn him of the consequences. However, when he came back to Krestinsky a little while later, Krestinsky once again rejected all Bessonov's evidence and once again declared that all his own evidence given to the preliminary investigation was untrue. Now he added pointedly that he could not tell the truth then because he was convinced that "until the judicial hearing took place, if there was to be one" he would be incapable of refuting the false evidence against him. "But why did you mislead the investigation and the public prosecutor's office?" Krestinsky replied, "I simply considered that if I were to say what I am saying today—that it was not in accordance with the facts—my declaration would not reach the leaders of the Party and the government." A few more questions were addressed by Krestinsky to Bessonov and then the morning session was declared closed. The adjournment between that and the evening session lasted for two hours.

The new evidence given by Krestinsky did indeed reach the leaders of the Party and government, and quickly. In the first place the accused were speaking into a microphone from which the cables ran not only to amplifiers within the hall itself but also to the Kremlin where Stalin was able to listen in on all the evidence sitting in his study. At various points around the hall secret microphones had also been installed for purposes of "controlling" the course of this most complicated performance. The whole trial from start to finish was also being recorded on film in the manner of a Party conference or one of the other important occasions worthy of being filmed from start to finish. Besides all this there is an enclosed balcony at the back of the October Hall. If anyone stands on that balcony his head can just be seen; anyone sitting there is invisible from the hall. From time to time a cloud of tobacco smoke from a cigarette or a pipe would rise above that balcony and several of the trial organizers and the correspondents were sure that Stalin kept dropping in for an hour or two to listen to and watch his assistants and opponents of recent times.

During the two-hour adjournment the whole "staff" of leading trial organizers met together in their special room. Since the present trial was such a great spectacle it was necessary for it to be under the control of an experienced producer accompanied by a group of deputies. This "staff" had long since been provided with comfortable quarters *underneath* the October Hall, the entry to which was carefully disguised, known only to the initiated, and closely guarded. The staff was headed by an old security man, one Zakovsky who had served in the *cheka* under Dzerzhinsky and Menzhinsky, moved up under Yagoda and retained his position under Yezhov. We have no means of telling what was said in discussion of the Krestinsky incident. After the adjournment Vyshinsky interrogated Rozengolts and Grinko, people's commissars—until their arrest—of foreign trade and finance. They gave the court all the "necessary" evidence including evidence which incriminated Krestinsky. The latter, however, continued to refute all the evidence and insist upon his innocence. Thus the first day of the trial was not a total success for its organizers. For several days after that the prosecutor refrained from interrogating Krestinsky and when, later on, it was his turn to be cross-examined he admitted every single charge leveled against him, confirming his "own" false evidence given during the preliminary investigation. But this was a different Krestinsky. There were people at the trial who knew the accused very well and could never have mistaken them. One of these people, discussing the trial with me, said, "On the first day of the trial it really was Krestinsky in the dock. Of course, Bukharin, Grinko, and Yagoda were there, and others that I had known well before. But next day in the dock sat a man who looked very much like Krestinsky but I could not have sworn that it really was him.

This was the only time during the trial when I doubted the identity of one of the accused." It seems quite probable that Krestinsky had been replaced by a cleverly made up actor. It is quite possible that for this show, as in any other theater, some roles were so important that they had permanent, or rapidly discovered, understudies.

The evidence given by Bukharin was not quite right. At the very least it provides food for thought. There seem to have been two planes to his evidence. For the man in the street it depicted an enemy of Stalin and of Soviet power, but the reflective researcher will find scattered throughout it many hints which cast doubt over the whole version of events presented by the court and the investigation. When confessing that he had belonged to the counter-revolutionary organization described as the "Rightist-Trotskyite Bloc" Bukharin observed that this organization had not sufficiently admitted its aims and crossed all the "t's." Confessing that he, Bukharin had led the "Rightist-Trotskyite Bloc," he observed that even as leader he could not have known the concrete details of what individual members of the bloc were about. Having claimed that the bloc which he had controlled had striven consciously for the restoration of capitalism in the Soviet Union, and that "we turned ourselves into vicious counterrevolutionaries, traitors, spies, and terrorists, we indulged in perfidy, crime, and treachery, we turned into a rebel unit . . .", etc., Bukharin simultaneously and unequivocally denied accusations of involvement in criminal attacks like the murder of Kirov, Menzhinsky, Gorky, and Kuibyshev. He was no less categorical in his denial of involvement in an attempt to murder Lenin in 1918, at a time when he had been leader of the "Left Communist" faction. On the subject of his journey abroad in the spring of 1936 Bukharin stated that this trip had helped him establish contact with Nicolaevsky who was close to the leadership of the Menshevik party. But from talking to Nicolaevsky Bukharin seemingly learned that he was already fully associated with agreements arrived at between the rightists, Zinovievites, Kamenev's men, and the Trotskyites and that he was familiar with Ryutin's platform. The only point agreed between Bukharin and Nicolaevsky was that the Mensheviks and the leaders of the Second International would initiate the necessary campaign in the press in the event of a collapse of the rightist center. A similar agreement was apparently reached also with the Socialist Revolutionary Mark Vishnyak, an ex-secretary of the Constituent Assembly.

After admitting at the outset that they had "all turned into spies" Bukharin suddenly claimed that he knew absolutely nothing about the espionage activities of the bloc. Even when Rykov, Sharangovich, and others had "confessed" to espionage and stated that Bukharin was *au fait* with their activities, he continued to assert that he had never indulged in espionage and knew not a thing about acts of espionage.

In giving a detailed account of his "contacts" with Trotsky and the Trotskyites and of his preparation of a coup d'état Bukharin, doubtlessly in full knowledge of what he was doing, committed a mass of contradictions in his evidence and, moreover, unequivocally refuted any connection between the "center" or "bloc" and White Guard or Fascist organizations. To the question of whether his group of associates had any connection with White Cossack circles in the Northern Caucasus Bukharin replied, "From the standpoint of mathematical probability one could say with a high degree of probability that that is a fact." Bukharin "remembered" that the "bloc" had agreed to Trotsky's proposal to give the Ukraine over to Fascist Germany but at the same time "forgot" that it was proposed also to hand over Belorussia along with the Ukraine. Bukharin totally refuted Khodzhayev's evidence of involvement with the British Secret Service. After many confessions of the most monstrous crimes Bukharin wound up by stating clearly that "confessions by the accused are not obligatory; confessions by the accused are a medieval principle of justice." This was stated with reference to a trial entirely constructed upon confessions by the accused. Although Bukharin, when he was being interrogated, agreed more often than not with the prosecution version of things, he did so almost always with reservations which irritated the prosecutor and the judges. At one session President Ulrikh could stand it no longer and said to Bukharin, "Yes, but you're going round and about; you're not saying anything about the crimes." Prosecutor Vyshinsky also said caustically to Bukharin at another stage of the interrogation, "You are obviously adopting a specific tactic, you will not tell the truth, you're hiding behind a torrent of words, quibbling over details, wandering off into politics, philosophy, theory, and so on, which you should forget once and for all, since you stand accused of espionage and, according to the facts of the investigation, you are a spy working for someone's intelligence service. So stop quibbling." The Soviet press confirmed during the trial that Bukharin was using one specific tactic—"attempting to use scientific-sounding phrases in order to confuse the prosecution, to obscure the truth and shield himself. In grand statements he proclaims himself responsible for everything and yet he refutes all the concrete accusations brought against him."[5]

The journal *October*, whose editorial board included writers like Zharov and Surkov who had taken issue so bitterly with Bukharin only recently at the First Congress of the Union of Soviet Writers, wrote in a leading article,

Bukharin . . . shambles up to the microphone as if preparing to deliver a routine pseudoscientific lecture. How skilled is this traitor in the art of disguising himself! Before the Revolution he wandered about, filling your heads with pernicious anarchist ideas. Austria, America, Japan . . . how are we to know what he did there? Was he not then privy to the secret hideouts and foxholes of intelligence services and the czarist secret police?

Well, the prosecutor asks him about this.

But the traitor is confused. He, of course, Bukharin, as leader, is responsible for everything, "everything in aggregate," but he cannot allow them to suspect him of working for the czarist secret police.

"If it suits you to ask questions like that."

But it *does* suit the prosecutor to ask them. He has every right to do so under the law; on the basis of the Soviet Criminal-Judiciary Code he is obliged to ask that question since Bukharin, pitiful loudmouth that he is, attempted to raise his hand against the great Lenin in 1918.

A damnable cross between a sow and a fox. A safe-breaker, a "bear-handler" turned political leader. A secret agent sets himself up to speak on "problems of leadership." . . .

An icy chill spread through the hall as the prosecutor asked accused Bukharin, "Did the leaders of the "Rightist Trotskyite Bloc" know of preparations for the murder of Kirov?" And then Bukharin, despite the evidence, despite all the testimony of his old friend Rykov, declares in an impassive professional voice, "I did not know of it."

Bukharin is lying as he has been doing for decades. He, believe it or not, has never sullied his "academic" little hands in the dirty doings of his neighbours in the dock. He is, if you please, only a man of ideas.

The others did the killing. The others did the wrecking. The others also did the spying. He just did the "interpreting," the analyzing of the bloody deeds committed by the people that he unleashed. He is a "theoretician." . . .

Seized by the hand, caught red-handed, Bukharin invokes Hegel to give false testimony, he plunges into a maze of linguistics and rhetoric, he mutters what sounds like scholarly words, anything just so long as he covers his tracks.[6]

At the morning session on 11 March 1938 Vyshinsky wound up for the prosecution and almost a third of his speech was devoted to the charges against Bukharin. For him and for most of the other accused he demanded the death penalty. The evening session and the whole of the following day (12 March) were given over to speeches for the defence made by I. D. Braude and N. V. Kommodov, which did not differ greatly from those of the prosecution, and to the last pleas of the accused. Even these sessions were not to pass without surprising incidents. A. P. Rosengolts, for instance, the ex-minister for foreign trade who had confessed to sabotage, espionage, the theft of government foreign currency which went to help Trotskyite activities and even joint-conspiracy along with Tukhachevsky, Uborevich, and Yakir to overthrow Soviet power by force of arms, suddenly launched into a recitation of the services he had performed during the October Revolution and the civil war —had he not incited the first military unit in Moscow to insurrection and then gone on to carry out the most complex of Party assignments in the very hardest regions of the civil war? Vyshinsky had asked for the death penalty for him too and Rozengolts declared that he was not asking for mitigation of such a severe sentence—that was something he did not deserve. But, he continued:

This does not mean that it is without a feeling of pain that I part with the beautiful land of the Soviets. We have beautiful new shoots now, a new generation reared by the Bolshevik party. We have such an upsurge in the Soviet Union as no other country in the world can boast. The pain of parting is intensified by the fact that we already have absolutely real results of socialist reconstruction. For the first time now we have a life, a full-blooded life, scintillating with joy and color. . . .

Then, to the amazement of everyone in the hall, Rozengolts followed these words by launching into song. He sang the famous ballad by Dunayevsky and Lebedev-Kumach which begins,

> O my homeland, broad and wide you stand,
> Field and forest, rivers fair to see.
> You are mine, I know no other land
> Where a man can live and breathe so free.

Most of those present, security personnel and the invited public, leaped to their feet, not knowing how best to react. Rozengolts, however, could not sing the song to the end. He broke off, choking with sobs, and sat down in his place.

Yagoda said his last few words to the court. He was still trying to deny that he had belonged to the central control group of the "bloc" or had been involved in organizing the murder of Kirov, though he did "confess" to other crimes. Finally, in a loud but faltering voice he said into the microphone, "Comrade Stalin! Comrades in the Security Office, spare me if you can!"

Bukharin continued the use of his earlier tactic even in his last plea. He admitted his guilt and assumed responsibility for all the "dastardly crimes committed by the Rightist-Trotskyite Bloc." But in the same breath he declared,

I have said, and I now repeat, that I was a leader and not a cog in the counterrevolutionary affairs. It follows from this, as will be clear to everybody, that there are many specific things which I could not have known, and which I actually did not know, but this does not relieve me of responsibility.

I admit that I am responsible, both politically and legally, for the defeatist orientation, for it did dominate in the "bloc of rightists and Trotskyites," although I affirm:

a) that personally I did not hold this position;

b) that the phrase about opening the front was not uttered by me. . . .

But I consider myself responsible for a grave and monstrous crime against the socialist fatherland and the whole international proletariat. I further consider myself responsible both politically and legally for wrecking activities, although I personally do not remember having given directions about wrecking activities. I did not talk about this. . . . Even in my testimony I mentioned that I had once told Radek that I considered this method of struggle as not very expedient. Yet Citizen, the state prosecutor makes me out to be a leader of the wrecking activities. . . .

Citizen, the procurator asserts that I was one of the major organizers of espionage, on a par with Rykov. What are the proofs? The testimony of Shavangovich, of whose existence I had not even heard until I read the indictment. . . .

Khodzhayev asserts that I advised him to get in contact with the British resident agent while Ikramov says that I told him that Turkestan was a choice morsel for England. In reality, this is far from the truth. I told Khodzhayev that advantage should be taken of the antagonism between the imperialist powers. . . .

I categorically deny my complicity in the assassination of Kirov, Menzhinsky, Kuybishev, Gorky, and Maksim Peshkov. According to Yagoda's testimony, Kirov was assassinated in accordance with a decision of the "Rightist-Trotskyite Bloc"; I knew nothing about it. . . .

For three months I refused to say anything. Then I began to testify. Why? Because while in prison I made a reevaluation of my entire past. For when you asked yourself: "If you must die, what are you dying for?"—an absolute black vacuity suddenly rises before you with startling vividness. . . . And, on the contrary, everything positive that glistens in the Soviet Union acquires new dimensions in a man's mind. This in the end disarmed me completely and led me to bend my knees before the Party and the country. . . .

The monstrousness of my crimes is immeasurable, especially in the new stage of the struggle of the USSR. . . .

It is in the consciousness of this that I await the verdict. What matters is not the personal feelings of the repentant enemy but the flourishing progress of the USSR and its international importance.[7]

Bukharin did not plead for clemency.

On the evening of 12 March, at a late hour, the court retired to the conference room and spent six hours considering the verdict. At 4:00 A.M. on the morning of 13 March the court reconvened and the weary public, guards, and accused resumed their places. Moscow was deserted. Outside the House of Unions no one was about. The legend that thousands of Muscovites were standing outside the court building awaiting the verdict has no basis in actuality.

It took about half an hour for the president of the court to read out the verdict, with everyone standing. Eighteen of the accused, including Bukharin, Rykov, Yagoda, Krestinsky, Rozengolts, Ivanov, Chernov, Grinko, Zelensky, Ikramov, and Khodzhayev were sentenced to "the supreme penalty—to be shot, with the confiscation of all their personal property." Dr. D. Pletnyov was sentenced to twenty-five years' imprisonment, while Rakovsky and Bessonov received twenty and fifteen years respectively.

On the night of 15 March 1938 Nikolai Bukharin, whom Lenin had once described as "deservedly the favourite of the Party," and also his comrades in misfortune were shot. It is known that prominent Party politicians whom Stalin knew personally were executed by shooting, or simply shot in the back of the neck, singly, in isolation. Stalin almost always took a sadistic pleasure in listening to the accounts given by the chief executioners of the last minutes of those people whom he had openly or secretly hated. We shall say nothing of the manner in which the other fellow-workers of Lenin bore themselves before their execution. As to Bukharin, he behaved with dignity. He did ask, however, to be given a pencil and paper in order to write a last letter to Stalin. His wish was granted. The note began with the words, "Koba, why do you need me to die?" Stalin kept this pre-execution letter from Bukharin all his life in one of the drawers of his desk along with a tart missive from Lenin about Stalin's crude behaviour toward Krupskaya and other similar documents.

The murder of Bukharin, Rykov, Krestinsky, and the others was but one atrocity in a whole series of terrible crimes committed by Stalin against the Party, against the Soviet people, against the Communist movement all over the world, which can never be forgotten and never shall be forgotten.

Instead of an Afterword

—————— ⇒⇒ ⇐⇐ ——————

THE ZINOVIEV-KAMENEV TRIAL in 1936 marked the beginning of a wave of repression, the innocent victims of which were to run into tens of thousands. The Piatakov-Radek trial in 1937 marked the beginning of a new, much more terrible wave of repression, the innocent victims of which ran into many hundreds of thousands. In January and February 1938 this ghastly terror began to abate slightly, though once the trial of Bukharin, Rykov, and the other accused was over the most vicious wave of all deluged our country and several million people became its victims. Almost every single Communist party in Comintern gave approval to this terror. The Soviet journal *Proletarian Revolution* summarized the Bukharin trial in 1938:

At this trial the mask was stripped off one of the vilest Jesuits and perfidious Pharisees ever known to history, Bukharin, the "theoretician." Neither his "scholarly" distortion nor his "philosophical" buffoonery enabled him to hide the genuine truth from the Soviet people. As early as the prewar period and during the Imperialist War Bukharin was a sworn enemy of Leninism, the author of provocational "leftist" slogans, an apologist for imperialism. A Trotskyite, he sang along with the others during the Great October Revolution. In 1918 he was involved in a counterrevolutionary plot against Lenin. Bukharin it was who spawned the dastardly plan to assassinate the leaders of the Revolution, Lenin, Stalin, and Sverdlov. Bukharin was the inspiration behind an attempt on the life of that great genius of humanity, Lenin, and he himself took part in it. Bukharin was a patron of the kulaks and a fervent proponent of the restoration of capitalism in the Soviet

Union. He spent the end of his vile life in a stinking underground organization accompanied by brigands and spies. Bukharin, this "damned cross between a sow and a vixen," a man who by his hypocrisy and slyness exceeded the slyest, most monstrous crimes ever known to history, was unmasked at this trial by his own fellow-conspirators.[1]

A new textbook on the history of the Bolshevik party, entitled *A Concise Course*, largely written by Stalin, was published in 1938. Here is an extract from it:

> The year 1937 uncovered new facts about the monsters in the Bukharin-Trotskyite gang. The trial in the case of Piatakov, Radek, and others, the trial in the case of Tukhachevsky, Yakir, and others, and finally the trial in the case of Bukharin, Rykov, Krestinsky, Rozengolts, and others—all these trials demonstrated that the Bukharinites and Trotskyites turned out to comprise one common gang of enemies in the form of a "Rightist-Trotskyite Bloc. . . ." These trials have made it manifest that the Trotskyite-Bukharinite monsters, as they carried out the orders of their masters, foreign intelligence services, aimed to destroy the Party and the Soviet state, to undermine the country's defences, to facilitate foreign military intervention and to work for the defeat of the Red Army and the dismantling of the Soviet Union . . . to restore capitalist slavery within the Soviet Union. . . . These White Guard pygmies who can only be compared in strength to paltry insects considered themselves, for the fun of it, masters of the country and fondly imagined that they could give away, or sell on the side, the Ukraine, Belorussia, and the sea states. . . . These worthless Fascist lackeys forgot that the Soviet people only has to stir a finger to remove them without trace. A Soviet court condemned the Bukharinite-Trotskyite monsters to death by shooting. The NKVD carried out the sentence. The Soviet people signified their approval of the destruction of the Bukharinite Trotskyite gang and then went about their business.[2]

Virtually every Communist party in every country of the world held a wave of meetings and published manifestoes in 1938 supporting the execution of Bukharin, Rykov, and their fellows. Take, for example, the French Communist party, whose leader Maurice Thorez stood up at one of the numerous workers' assemblies on 3 June 1938 and spoke as follows:

> Justice in the Soviet Union has performed a service of inestimable value in the cause of peace by striking down without mercy those Trotskyite-Bukharinite traitors, murderers, and Gestapo agents, those "fifth column"

elements, those canting hypocrites, mourned by one or two people in England, for having been punished with the necessary severity.[3]

A large group of Communist and members of the Communist Youth movement sent a telegram to Yezhov in the spring of 1938. Part of it read,

> Your resolution and your unbending will have led to the exposure of vile agents of fascism. . . . Please be assured of our total confidence in the justice of the people who have punished the traitors according to their deserts.[4]

More than forty years have passed since the day, or rather the night, of Bukharin's murder. It is impossible to calculate all that has happened throughout these years which has had at least an indirect association with "the case of Bukharin." Soon after the trial Anna Larina, Bukharin's wife, was brought back to Moscow from Astrakhan. At the Lubyanka she was subjected to interminable interrogation. She spent all but six months in the "water cell"—a small cell permanently ankle-deep in cold water. Only her youth and fitness enabled Larina to survive this torture. When Yezhov was replaced Beria took over the interrogation. She spent the next eighteen years in the camps and in exile. She was rehabilitated only after the Twentieth Party Congress. Bukharin's small son was brought up by Anna's sister who lived in the Urals. For almost twenty years he had no idea who his mother and father were. Now they live in Moscow and for many years, so far without success, they have been working for the formal rehabilitation of Nikolai Bukharin, applying to each successive Communist Party Congress, to the Central Committee, and the USSR Supreme Soviet. To all intents and purposes the political trial of 1938 has long since been exposed for what it was and full rehabilitation has been granted to Krestinsky, Ivanov, Chernov, Grinko, Zelensky, Ikramov, Khodzhayev, and one or two others among the accused at that trial. By now quite a number of articles on these people have appeared in the Soviet press and sketches and pamphlets about them have appeared. At the All-Union Conference of Historians in December 1962 the then secretary of the Central Committee, Pyotr Pospelov, answering questions from the platform, said,

> I can state that a careful study of the papers of the Twenty-second Communist Party Congress is sufficient to determine that, of course, neither Bukharin nor Rykov was ever a spy or terrorist.[5]

However, in the face of all logic, Bukharin and Rykov have still never been rehabilitated in state or Party terms and the sentence passed on them on 13 March 1938 has yet to be formally annulled. This is not to say that the possibility has never been discussed. After the Twentieth Party Congress the question of a formal annulment of these sentences, plus those passed in the trials of 1936 and '37 was considered by the Central Committee presidium. It was decided to rehabilitate the so-called military group, that is Tukhachevsky, Yakir, Uborevich, and others who were shot following the closed trial of 1937. Their rehabilitation occurred in 1957, precisely twenty years after the execution. The possible rehabilitation of Bukharin, Zinoviev, and Kamenev was an issue which evoked passionate debate. Other people were involved including prominent leaders of the Communist movement abroad, such as Maurice Thorez and Harry Pollit. Thorez flew to Moscow and strongly urged Khrushchev to resist the temptation to annul the 1936–38 sentences. "After the Twentieth Party Congress and the events in Hungary," he pointed out, "more than 100,000 members have left the party. Rehabilitate these people one by one, say one a month." Khrushchev gave in to this pressure and regretted it ever afterwards.

Winding up for the prosecution on 11 March 1938 Vyshinsky had closed with these words:

> Time will pass. The graves of the hateful traitors will grow over with weeds and thistle, they will be covered with the eternal contempt of honest Soviet citizens, of the entire Soviet people. But over us, over our happy country, our sun will shine with its luminous rays as bright and joyous as before. Over the road cleared of the last scum and filth of the past, we, our people with our beloved leader and teacher, the great Stalin, at our head, will march as before onwards and onwards, toward communism!

There are a lot of mistakes here. Bukharin, and most of the other accused who were executed with him, have not been forgotten by the Soviet people. There are many Old Bolsheviks and Communist Youth members of the 1920s who still remember Bukharin with the greatest respect. He has not been forgotten as a contributor to the international Communist movement. Many Western Communist parties do not need to have Bukharin rehabilitated; they write about him and speak of him as one of the worthiest figures in the Russian Revolution. In our country, however, those who work in ideological institutions or teach political economy, Party history, or allied sociological disciplines know virtually nothing of Bukharin as theoretician, or ideologue or as a prominent leader of the Bolshevik party and the Comintern. The large number of books, pamphlets, and articles written by Bukharin are quite inaccessible to us.

We have no desire to overestimate the theoretical legacy inherited from Bukharin. Some of his works are clearly obsolete, a number of his predictions have not come true, and part of his work may now appear inchoate or superficial. This is, of course, the fate of all theoreticians, even the greatest. Bukharin created no complete and independently conceived new theories. He attempted to extend the theoretical curiosity of Lenin in the area of the construction of socialism, and to explore all possible paths for the development of the Soviet state with the aim of discovering an alternative to the proposals made by the "leftists," which he found repulsive, for a tightening of the dictatorship of the proletariat and an intensification of the class struggle.

Sidney Heitman is correct when he says,

Although the abandonment of NEP and the inauguration of the First Five Year Plan signalled the end of the brief stage of Soviet history identified with Bukharin's predominance in the Party, an understanding of this period and of Bukharin's role during it is important for several reasons. . . . Bukharin's response to the basic ideological issues of the nineteen-twenties provides unique insight into the problems confronting the Bolshevik leadership during the first formative decade of Soviet rule, when the question of Russia's future was still unresolved and susceptible to alternative solutions. Following Stalin's rise to unrivalled power, he effectively denied this fact by depicting the history of the Party as something predetermined, in the course of which there had always been only one canonical line of orthodox doctrinal descent running from Marx through Lenin to himself. A better knowledge of Bukharin's role in the history of the nineteen-twenties and particularly of his theory of building socialism in Russia during these years may not only help to dispel further the Stalinist myths, but also provide greater understanding of the true nature of the issues and of the possible courses open to the Party before 1928. . . .

It may be noted that had Bukharin's views rather than Stalin's prevailed after 1928, they would have yielded radically different results than those that followed from Stalin's course. While it may be futile to speculate on what might have been, since history consists only of what in fact occurred, nonetheless a comparison of the projected implications of Bukharin's gradualist theory of socialist construction with the manifest consequences of Stalin's may provide considerable insight into the inherent nature of Communism and illuminate the perplexing question of how one of the most humane and idealistic doctrines in all of history was transformed into a tragic perversion of itself and bent to the service of one of the cruellest tyrannies in all of history.[6]

There is a lot of truth in these words. In the east and in the west the world still manages to make its way down the path of socialism. It is no easy path. However, if we fail to study and analyze those actual events, those difficulties and contradictions which have been encountered along that path then we can only multiply the difficulties which today confront all the peoples of our planet.

In the last analysis Vyshinsky was not entirely wrong. Even today, so many years after the Twentieth and even the Twenty-second Party Congress, when the whole world is aware of the monstrous crimes committed by Stalin, one of which was the murder of Bukharin, we do not even know where this prominent member of the Bolshevik party is buried. We do know where they buried his accuser, A. Ya. Vyshinsky, one of the most sinister figures of the Stalin era. Vyshinsky died in late 1954 and was accorded a solemn funeral in Red Square. His ashes are at rest in the Kremlin wall not far from Lenin's tomb. And the inscription there which bears his name seems to serve as a reminder that not every last vestige of the evil of Stalinism has yet disappeared into our country's past history.

Notes

———— »» «« ————

FOREWORD

1. V. I. Lenin, *Polnoye sobraniye so-chineniy,* vol. 36, p. 303.
2. Op. cit., vol. 34, p. 533.
3. N. I. Bukharin, *The Path to Socialism*

in Russia [*Put' k Sotsializmu v Rossii*], ed. S. Heitman, (New York: Omicron Books, 1967), pp. 37–39.

One / ON THE THRESHOLD OF A NEW DECADE

1. J. Stalin, *Sobraniye sochineniy,* vol. 11, p. 318.
2. Ibid., p. 260.
3. *Bolshevik,* No. 2, 1930, p. 8.
4. D. Bedny, *Sobraniye sochineniy,* vol. IV, (Moscow-Leningrad, 1926), 35–36.

5. Stalin, op. cit., vol. 12, p. 1.
6. V. Katanyan, "Iz vospominaniy," *Ros-siya,* No. 3 (Turin, 1977), pp. 177–8.
7. Ibid., pp. 181–2.

Two / THE SIXTEENTH PARTY CONGRESS

1. *XVI s'yezd VKP(B), Stenograficheskiy otchet* (Moscow, 1931), p. 109.
2. Ibid., p. 134.
3. Ibid., p. 157–8.
4. Ibid., p. 209.
5. Ibid., p. 142.

6. Ibid., p. 149.
7. Ibid., p. 155.
8. Ibid., p. 157.
9. Ibid., p. 178.
10. Ibid., p. 213.
11. Ibid., p. 299.

Three / NIKOLAI BUKHARIN: 1931–33

1. *Sorena,* No. 1 (Moscow, 1931), pp. 4–5.
2. From the unpublished memoirs of A. Khrabrovitsky.
3. From the unpublished memoirs of E. P. Frolov.
4. N. Mandelstam, *Vospominaniya,* (New York: Chekhov Publishing House, 1970), pp. 120–23.

5. *Pravda,* 29 March 1928.
6. *Izvestiya,* 29 December 1933.
7. V. I. Lenin, *Zamechaniya na stat'i N. I. Bukharina o gosudarstve,* (Party Publishing House: Moscow, 1933), pp. 18–19.
8. Ibid., pp. 6–7.

Four / THE SEVENTEENTH PARTY CONGRESS

1. *Pravda*, 14 January 1933.
2. *XVII s'yezd VKP(B)*, *Stenografiches-*

kiy otchet (Moscow, 1934), pp. 124–5.
3. Ibid., pp. 127–8.

Five / NIKOLAI BUKHARIN AS EDITOR OF *IZVESTIYA*

1. From Baitalsky's unpublished memoirs. See *Politicheskiy dnevnik*, vol. 1 (Herzen Fund: Amsterdam, 1972), pp. 547–8.
2. N. Mandelstam, *Vospominaniya*, (New York: Chekhov Publishing House, 1970), pp. 24–26.

Six / THE FIRST CONGRESS OF SOVIET WRITERS

1. *Literaturnaya entsiklopediya*, vol. 1 (Moscow, 1929), pp. 631–3.
2. *Pervyy s'yezd sovetskikh pisateley, stenograficheskiy otchet (Moscow, 1934)*, p. 480.
3. Ibid., p. 498.
4. Ibid., p. 503.
5. I. Berger, *Krusheniye pokoleniya* (Florence, 1973), p. 138.
6. *Pervyy s'yezd sovetskikh pisateley, stenograficheskiy otchet* (Moscow, 1934), p. 512.
7. Ibid., pp. 513–14.
8. Ibid., p. 514.
9. Ibid., p. 524.
10. Ibid., p. 536.
11. Ibid., p. 550.
12. Ibid., p. 551.
13. J. Stalin, *Sochineniya*, vol. 13, pp. 23–27.
14. *Pervyy s'yezd sovetskikh pisateley, stenograficheskiy otchet* (Moscow, 1934), p. 557.
15. Ibid., pp. 558–9.
16. Ibid., p. 564.
17. Ibid., p. 573.
18. Ibid., p. 577.
19. Ibid., p. 479.
20. Ibid., p. 513.
21. Ibid., p. 574.
22. Ibid., p. 671.
23. *Novy Mir*, No. 10, 1966, p. 258.
24. *Kratkaya literaturnaya entsiklopediya*, vol. 7 (Moscow, 1972), p. 289.
25. *Pervyy s'yezd sovetskikh pisateley, stenograficheskiy otchet* (Moscow, 1934), p. 490.
26. Ibid., pp. 490–91.

Seven / NIKOLAI BUKHARIN: DECEMBER 1934 TO FEBRUARY 1936

1. V. I. Lenin, *Polnoye sobraniye sochineniy*, vol. 6, p. 15.
2. Ibid., vol. 44, p. 398.
3. Ibid., p. 365.
4. Ibid., vol. 45, p. 13.
5. Ibid., pp. 3–4.
6. Ibid., vol. 43, p. 228.
7. *Izvestiya*, 30 January 1936.

Eight / ABROAD

1. The Marx-Engels Institute, established in 1922, was directed by the USSR Central Executive Committee from 1924 onwards. After Lenin's death the Party Central Committee set up the Lenin Institute charged with the task of publishing his complete works. In the early 1930s the two institutes were brought together to form the Marx-Engels-Lenin Institute (IMEL).
2. *Politicheskiy dnevnik*, (Herzen Fund: Amsterdam, 1972), pp. 154–64.
3. B. I. Nicolaevsky, *Power and the Soviet Élite*, ed. Janet D. Zagoria (London, 1966), pp. 11–13.

Nine / THE DIFFICULT SUMMER AND ARDUOUS AUTUMN OF 1936

No notes.

Ten / THE LAST WEEKS OF FREEDOM

1. *Izvestiya*, 30 January 1937.

Eleven / THE INVESTIGATION

1. I. Berger, *Krusheniye pokoleniya* (Florence, 1973), pp. 140–41.
2. M. Ioffe, *One Long Night*, tr. V. Dixon (New York, 1977), pp. 72–73.
3. A. Koestler, *Darkness at Noon* tr. D. Hardy (London: Hutchinson, Danube Edition, 1973), p. 183.
4. Ibid., p. 224.
5. Ibid., pp. 224–7.
6. Ibid., pp. 227–8.
7. *Vestnik akademii nauk*, No. 6, 1937, p. 76.

Twelve / THE TRIAL

1. A. Solzhenitsyn, *The Gulag Archipelago 1918–56*, tr. T. P. Whitney (London, 1974), p. 408.
2. Ibid., p. 134.
3. Ibid., pp. 141–2.
4. See, for example, Davies's letter to his daughter of 8 March (five days before sentencing), in which he states, "All the fundamental weaknesses and vices of human nature—personal ambitions at their worst—are shown up in the proceedings. They disclose the outlines of a plot which came very near to being successful in bringing about the overthrow of this government." After the trial he wrote in confidence to the secretary of state (17 March), "it is my opinion so far as the political defendants are concerned sufficient crimes . . . were established . . . beyond a reasonable doubt to justify the verdict of guilty of treason. . . ." Joseph E. Davies, *Mission to Moscow* (London, 1943), pp. 177–79.
5. *Izvestiya*, 9 March 1938.
6. *Oktyabr'*, No. 3, 1938, pp. 5–6.
7. *Izvestiya*, 13 March 1938.

INSTEAD OF AN AFTERWORD

1. *Proletarskaya Revolyutsiya*, 1938, No. 9, p. 10.
2. *Istoriya Komunisticheskoy Partii (Bolsheviki)*, *Kratkiy Kurs* (Moscow, 1938), pp. 331–2.
3. *Kommunisticheskiy Internatsional*, No. 5, 1938, p. 39.
4. Ibid., No. 4, p. 127.
5. *Vsesoyuznoye Soveshchaniye Istorikov*, 'Nauka' Edition (Moscow, 1964), p. 298.
6. N. I. Bukharin, *The Path to Socialism in Russia [Put' k Sotsializmu v Rossii]*, ed. S. Heitman (New York: Omicron Books, 1967), pp. 49–50.

Index